Is Philosophy Androcentric?

Is Philosophy Androcentric?

IDDO LANDAU

THE PENNSYLVANIA STATE UNIVERSITY PRESS
UNIVERSITY PARK, PENNSYLVANIA

library of congress
cataloging-in-publication data

Landau, Iddo, 1958–
    Is philosophy androcentric? / by Iddo Landau.
        p.   cm.
Includes bibliographical references and index.
ISBN 0-271-02906-4 (cloth : alk. paper)
1. Philosophy.
2. Men—Attitudes.
3. Androcentrism.
4. Feminist theory.
I. Title.

B53.L32 2006
108.2—dc22
2006005752

Contents

Acknowledgments

This book owes a great deal to many people. Its origins go back many years to when I was a graduate student at McGill and was first exposed to arguments for the androcentricity of philosophy, which led to stimulating discussions with teachers and friends. I am especially grateful to Frieda Forman, who first introduced me to the literature and helped me understand some difficult issues. Her passion for the subject, and for philosophizing in general, has influenced this book in numerous ways.

Many people have been warmly supportive of the project and very generously gave of their time to reading and commenting on the whole manuscript. I am greatly indebted to Jean Bethke Elshtain, Gal Gerson, Bob Goodman, Agnes Heller, Annabel Herzog, Mary Hesse, Ivor Ludlam, Arlene Saxonhouse, Danny Statman, and Mary Warnock for their many helpful comments, questions, and criticisms, which alerted me to problems, and helped me correct various mistakes.

Part of the research for and the writing of this book took place during my sabbatical at Oxford in the academic year 2000–2001. I am grateful to St. John's College, Oxford, for granting me membership in its Senior Common room for the year. During that year I came to know two people who became friends. My conversations with Peter Hacker have been a source of pleasure and intellectual stimulation for me through the years, and I have gained from them a great deal. I have learned much from and also enjoyed thoroughly my meetings and discussions with the late Ossie Hanfling. Ossie's sudden death, while the book was being prepared for publication, was a great blow. His many knowledgeable suggestions and constructive questions compelled me to clarify numerous points and helped improve the book in many ways.

The two readers appointed by Penn State University Press, Sara Worley and Harriet Baber (who helpfully commented on two drafts of the book), made excellent suggestions. I am grateful to them for their time and thoughtfulness. Sandy Thatcher, editor and director at Penn State University Press, was supportive and efficient throughout the process of refereeing and improving the book. I am very grateful to him.

One other person volunteered to read two drafts of the book. Saul Smilansky, a very close friend for years, has been a constant source of wise advice, unfailing support, and perceptive (and frequently funny) comments. I owe a lot to Saul's friendship. The generosity and intellectual honesty of all the people mentioned here emerges as all the more striking once it is remembered that many of them do not agree, and several strongly disagree, with some of the arguments presented in this book. Of course, the responsibility for the claims made here rests with me alone.

Issues discussed in the book arose in my graduate seminars at the University of Haifa. I am indebted to my students for their helpful criticism, and most of all to Sara Cohen Shabot, Anat Gelber, Noemi Harari, Yaki Menschenfreund, Ishai Ron, and Lotem Rotbain-Sher. Hilla Polak, Sergei Talenker, and Oren Yaqobi helped with various research missions. Stuart Cornfield, Mira Reich, Danna Rothman, Glendyr Sacks, Marion Lupu, and Andrew B. Lewis, a copyeditor for the press, greatly enhanced the style of the book with the comments and revisions they suggested. I am very grateful to them all.

Certain chapters in the book make use of materials from my own articles. I gratefully acknowledge the permission of journals to use materials from the following articles: "Early and Later Deconstruction in the Writings of Jacques Derrida," © *Cardozo Law Review,* originally published in 14 CARDOZO L. REV. 1895 (1993); "Should There Be Separatist Feminist Epistemologies?" *The Monist* 77 (1994): 462–71, Copyright © 1994, *The Monist*: An International Quarterly Journal of General Philosophical Inquiry, reprinted by permission; "How Androcentric Is Western Philosophy?" *The Philosophical Quarterly* (Blackwell Publishing) 46 (1996): 48–59; "Mendus on Philosophy and Pervasiveness," *The Philosophical Quarterly* (Blackwell Publishing) 47 (1997): 89–93; and "Feminist Criticisms of Metaphors in Bacon's Philosophy of Science," *Philosophy* 73 (1998): 47–61.

My greatest debt is to the love and support of my family: my wife, Yael, our children Uri and Tommer, my sister, Ronit, and my parents, Zipora and Jacob M. Landau. The book is dedicated to my parents, with love.

I.L.

1

Introduction

Some might also consider it unwise to analyze contemporary feminists with the same seriousness and detail as I do in my exploration of the "greats." There will be feminist readers, on the other hand, who will remain unconvinced that "patriarchal theorists" should be given sympathetic consideration at all. Should these two sorts of criticisms arise I would not be surprised: each of us prefers that someone other than ourselves, or those thinkers, or that tradition or movement to which we are committed, be the subject of critique.

—Jean Bethke Elshtain, *Public Man, Private Woman*

I

The claim has often been made that Western philosophy is androcentric, that is, that it should be reformed or rejected because it suits men's experiences or minds more than women's, or involves male discrimination against women, or leads to the domination of women by men. Thus, for example, Morwenna Griffiths and Margaret Whitford write: "The practice and content of Western philosophy are male-dominated and male-biased. This statement is not directed at any one set of philosophers. It is true in general, in spite of the fact that philosophers by no means speak with a single voice, and do not even agree among themselves about what they understand philosophy to be."[1] And Jane Flax asserts that "philosophy reflects the fundamental division of the world according to gender and a fear and devaluation of women characteristic of patriarchal attitudes."[2]

Such claims abound, since as Alison M. Jaggar and Iris Marion Young argue, feminist philosophy "has moved to investigating the overt and covert ways in which the devaluation of women may be inherent in the most enduring ideals, the central concepts, and the dominant theories of philosophy,"[3] and as Genevieve Lloyd explains, feminist history of philosophy "has . . . been largely concerned with critique of the 'male' assumptions of past philosophy."[4] Some theorists also believe that West-

1. "Introduction," 1–2.
2. "Political Philosophy," 268.
3. "Introduction," 1.
4. "Feminism in History of Philosophy," 249.

ern philosophy (like other fields of Western knowledge) is so androcentric that a thorough, pervasive philosophical or cognitive-scientific revolution is needed. Sandra Harding and Merrill Hintikka, for example, write that "we cannot understand women and their lives by adding facts about them to bodies of knowledge which take men, their lives, and their beliefs as the human norm." Part of the reason for this is that "the attempts to add understandings of women to our knowledge of nature and social life have led to the realization that there is precious little reliable knowledge to which to add them."[5] Laura Lyn Inglis and Peter K. Steinfeld argue that "feminist philosophy must become self-conscious in the appropriation of patriarchal texts. To do so requires a way, a path, a hermeneutical method. We propose that this hermeneutical method be informed by and infused with subversion . . . that can transform the whole of the past."[6] And Phyllis Rooney asserts that "the . . . struggle to create a world that encourages women to their full expression in words and action must be supported by nothing short of the remythologizing of voice and agency and the remythologizing of reason, emotion, intuition, and nature."[7] This also seems to be what Sandra Harding has in mind when she writes that "I doubt that in our wildest dreams we ever imagined we would have to reinvent both science and theorizing itself in order to make sense of women's social experience."[8] There are many further expressions of the view that takes philosophy, or even more generally, knowledge, theory, or culture as a whole, to be androcentric, and as such requiring reform or rejection, and sees "feminism's philosophical task as finding a truly feminine counterpart to an irredeemably masculinist tradition."[9]

The feminist discussion of the androcentricity of philosophy is significant for our view and understanding of philosophy. The present study aims to add to this discussion; it supports a version of what now is still a minority position and argues that philosophy is androcentric but in many aspects less so than frequently claimed. The discussion suggests that philosophy is, in most respects and ways, not androcentric, and that

5. "Introduction," ix.
6. *Old Dead White Men's Philosophy*, xiv.
7. "Gendered Reason," 96.
8. *Science Question in Feminism*, 251.
9. I am quoting from Fricker and Hornsby, "Introduction," 4. Fricker and Hornsby themselves, however, do not take this to be an appropriate task for feminist philosophy. For more examples of the call for a pervasive feminist philosophical revolution, see Chapter 9.

the few ways in which it is androcentric are less consequential than is frequently believed.

2

Feminist philosophy, which appeared in the late 1960s as one of the many branches of women's studies, has dealt with questions concerning the androcentricity of philosophy from its very start. But this was only one of a variety of issues that feminist philosophers, and feminists in general, took an interest in. Feminist philosophy also dealt with, for instance, questions in political and moral philosophy that carry special importance to women (such as abortion, affirmative action, and sexual harassment), critiques of androcentric claims, and acknowledgment and analysis of important but unnoticed works of women philosophers. At first, discussions of the androcentricity of philosophy were quite limited in scope and mostly focused on explicit androcentric remarks found in philosophical texts (such as Aristotle's claim that women are less rational than men, or Kant's assertion that women should not be allowed to vote). With time, however, the arguments for the androcentricity of philosophy started dealing also with basic norms, structures, and methodologies and presented wider and more condemning conclusions concerning the extent and depth of the androcentricity of philosophy. (Thus, in some cases, mainstream philosophy has come to be referred to, tongue in cheek, as "malestream" philosophy.) Many of the important arguments for the androcentricity of philosophy appeared in the 1980s and early 1990s, dominating the feminist discussion of this topic to the present, drawing interest and gaining approval in many (though by no means all) feminist philosophical circles.

These changes did not occur, of course, in a vacuum; they were partly influenced by, and in turn influenced, tendencies in modern Continental philosophy such as postmodernism, the Frankfurt School, and philosophical critical theory. Some of the arguments for the androcentricity of philosophy may be seen as part of the ongoing criticism that these interrelated movements have directed at traditional philosophy or at analytic philosophy. In spite of this mutual influence and relevance, however, it should be noted that even the feminist discussions with stronger links to modern Continental work have their own subject matter and perspective (having to do with women), and that many arguments and claims for the androcentricity of philosophy have been presented independently of the modern Continental tradition. Although some elements of the discussion of the androcentricity of philosophy can be seen as part of a larger dispute, others have a character of their own.

These observations relate to some possible misunderstandings about the purpose and scope of this book, which I am eager to dissolve from the very start. The book focuses on the question of the androcentricity of Western philosophy, and on this issue alone. Thus, it does not deal with general questions in modern Continental philosophy, although some of the critiques of arguments for the androcentricity of philosophy might also have some bearing on these questions. Similarly, it does not discuss the question of androcentricity in non-Western philosophy, or in disciplines outside philosophy, although, again, some of its comments might prove to be partly relevant for other fields and for non-Western philosophy. Likewise, some critiques of arguments for the androcentricity of philosophy are applicable—with suitable modifications—to some arguments for the Eurocentricity of philosophy and thought. These too are beyond the scope of this work.

Moreover, since it focuses only on the question of the androcentricity of philosophy, the book does not discuss other issues in feminist philosophy, a fortiori, issues in other parts of feminist studies.

It would also be incorrect to assume that all or almost all feminist theorists have taken philosophy to be androcentric, or pervasively androcentric. This impression may arise because, as mentioned above, since the 1980s, the contention that Western philosophy is androcentric has been widely accepted in many feminist philosophical circles, and the androcentricity of Western philosophy, or the need to create alternatives to it, has been commonly discussed. Moreover, many of the authors of these arguments are some of the most important and frequently cited figures in feminist theory, such as (in alphabetical order) Susan Bordo, Lorraine Code, Jane Flax, Carol Gilligan, Sandra Harding, Nancy Hartsock, Luce Irigaray, Evelyn Fox Keller, Genevieve Lloyd, Audre Lorde, Catharine MacKinnon, Susan Mendus, Carole Pateman, Phyllis Rooney, and Naomi Scheman. However, feminist philosophy is a highly diverse intellectual movement and includes a wide spectrum of different and sometimes conflicting attitudes. While many feminist philosophers support the view that philosophy is androcentric, others criticize different aspects of this view.[10] Others show their rejection of various claims for the andro-

10. See, for example, Antony, "Is Psychological Individualism a Piece of Ideology?"; Atherton, "Cartesian Reason and Gendered Reason"; Baier, "Hume: The Reflective Women's Epistemologist?"; Elshtain, "Contesting Care"; Grimshaw, *Philosophy and Feminist*

centricity of philosophy in the way they philosophize, or in their uses of the philosophical tradition to strengthen and develop feminist positions. The majority of feminist philosophers seem to accept certain arguments for the androcentricity of philosophy, but not others, and only to a certain extent, but not further. Moreover, in recent years there seems to have grown in feminist philosophy a slow but persistent discomfort about many of the claims for the androcentricity of philosophy.[11] This discomfort, however, has not yet expressed itself in a comprehensive discussion such as the one suggested here.

Yet another misconception that should be addressed from the start is that showing Western philosophy to be less androcentric than is sometimes claimed involves an attempt to show that feminism is misguided in general. This again would be mistaken, not only because of the variety of feminist philosophical views about the androcentricity of philosophy, but also because the central general objective of feminism—liberating women and bringing an end to the systematic injustice done to them— does not depend on the claim that philosophy is androcentric. Nor is the tenability of almost all specific feminist objectives and claims affected in any way by a discussion of the androcentricity of philosophy.

Yet another possible misconception that might arise here is that this book proposes to evaluate and critique feminist *scholarship*. Since I aim to show that Western philosophy is less androcentric than is frequently portrayed, I often focus on what I take to be problematic in arguments for the androcentricity of philosophy. However, such an emphasis— typical of a polemical work—should not be understood as making a point about the level of feminist scholarship, more than, say, the arguments presented in the liberalism/communitarianism debate, or scientific realism/anti-realism debate, or, within feminist theory, the disagreements between those supporting and those opposing the legalization of prostitution should be understood as making a point about the level of scholarship of the sides of these debates.

Thinking; Haack, *Manifesto of a Passionate Moderate,* esp. preface and chaps. 6, 7, 10, and 11; Hampton, "Feminist Contractarianism"; Herman, "Kant on Sex and Marriage"; Lovibond, "Feminism and the 'Crisis of Rationality'"; Nussbaum, "Feminist Critique of Liberalism"; and Richards, *Sceptical Feminist,* esp. chaps. 1–4. This, of course, is not an exhaustive list of feminist philosophers and works that criticize different versions of the claim that philosophy is androcentric.

11. Cf. Lloyd, "Feminism in History of Philosophy," 245: Although "the history of philosophy was seen as a repository of misogynist ideas and ideals, towards which feminism took up a defensive posture," "in more recent work inspired by feminism, a more positive mood is evident." (Yet in the same article Lloyd also mentions "the undoubtedly 'male' past of philosophy" [261].)

The last possible misunderstanding that I would like to refer to at this point is that the book aims to present an overview, or a survey, of the different feminist views on the androcentricity question. This would misconstrue the book, however, for it does not aim to map the domain, but rather to make a case for a certain position, and for that purpose it presents, and critiques, arguments supporting the other position.

3

The nature of the question asked in this study should be clearly set out. It is presupposed here that one of our main activities in dealing with philosophical views is determining which of them we agree with, agree with only after modifications, or reject. We may or may not decide to employ, say, Plato's theory of universals, Proclus' theory of the mystical union, Wittgenstein's theory of language, or Rawls's theory of justice as theories that explain to us how the world is or how we should act in it. To make such decisions we use a variety of considerations. Among these, we may decide to reject, or to accept only after some modifications, a philosophical theory because we believe that it suits men's experiences or minds more than women's, or involves male discrimination against women, or leads to the domination of women by men. In such a case, we may call this theory "androcentric."[12]

The term "androcentric," then, is used here not only descriptively, as what "suits men's experiences or minds more than women's, or involves male discrimination against women, or leads to the domination of women by men," but also normatively, as what *should be rejected, or reformed,* because it suits men's experiences or minds more than women's, or involves male discrimination against women, or leads to the domination of women by men."[13] It does not merely describe notions or philosophies as suiting men's minds more than women's, or involving male discrimination against women, but also calls for rejecting or reform-

12. Some other terms employed in the literature are "male," "male chauvinist," "malestream," "patriarchal," "sexist," "misogynist," "phallocentric," "phallogocentric," and "masculine" or "masculinist." Such terms rarely appear in this work, and when they do they are used interchangeably with "androcentric."

13. To some, the distinction may appear superfluous; it may seem that whatever satisfies the descriptive criterion of androcentricity also satisfies the normative one. I argue in Chapters 3 and 7, however, that there may be philosophies that suit men's minds more than women's, yet are not androcentric.

ing such philosophies.[14] The question asked in this study is operative: can we—arguments to the contrary notwithstanding—continue to employ philosophy as it is, or should we reject or reform it because of its putative androcentricity?

Philosophy, or a philosophy, may be taken to be pervasively androcentric (that is, requiring rejection or replacement by feminist alternatives of most of its theses and aspects), or nonpervasively androcentric (that is, allowing most of it to remain unchanged by requiring merely a renunciation of some androcentric themes and, if necessary, a few other connected themes).[15] I suggest in this study that none of the arguments for the androcentricity of philosophy shows that it is pervasively androcentric, and that only a few arguments show philosophy to be nonpervasively androcentric.

The question discussed in this book—whether we can continue to employ philosophy as it is or have to reject or reform it because of its putative androcentricity—should be distinguished from other questions. The study does not inquire whether or not philosophy (or a certain philosophical theory) should be reformed or rejected, but whether or not it should be reformed or rejected because it is *androcentric.* There are many other reasons—for example, logical, factual, moral—for accepting, reforming, or rejecting philosophical theories. These, however, are outside the scope of the present work. For the same reason, when the discussion leads to the conclusion that a certain philosophical theory or view is not androcentric, this does not imply that that theory should be accepted, but only that it should not be rejected or modified because of considerations *pertaining to androcentricity.* The book is limited, then, to a discussion of philosophy and androcentricity and does not follow studies that combine their arguments for the androcentricity of philosophical views with arguments about other difficulties in the views they discuss.[16]

The question discussed here should also be distinguished from that pertaining to the blameworthiness of those philosophers who express androcentric views. Some authors consider whether or not these philosophers could have known better, could have avoided being influenced by

14. Thus, I assume in this discussion that androcentric claims, notions, and so on, should be rejected. I also presuppose in this study that androcentric claims, as well as claims that are sufficient conditions to androcentric claims, are untrue.

15. The distinction is of degree rather than of kind, and admits some borderline cases that are difficult to classify.

16. See, for example, Hornsby, "Feminism in Philosophy of Language," 93, 95, and Code, *What Can She Know?* 29, 30, 33, 37–38, 41, 47.

views predominant in their time, and so on.[17] These questions, too, are distinct from the one examined here, which is whether, or to what extent, we have reason to reject or reform philosophies on account of their androcentricity.[18]

The discussion presupposes that theories and views written in the past can be relevant to us today, and that there is a point in discussing whether we, at present, should accept, accept in an amended form, or completely reject philosophies and views devised in the past by, say, Aristotle, Hume, or Kant. In this, the book follows the arguments for the androcentricity of philosophy that it examines: they too presuppose that there is a point in discussing whether such philosophies should be rejected or accepted, and they too apply recent, gender-related criteria to older theories. Note that the book does not ask whether the views or theories it discusses were androcentric in the past, but whether they are androcentric today, namely, whether we, today, can accept (as related to the androcentricity question) these philosophies and views, or need to reform or discard them.[19]

This is perhaps also the place to refer to the way I employ "philosophy" in this book. I do not intend to define the field (doing so satisfactorily would require considerable digression), and assume that the reader is familiar with the way the notion is commonly used today, which is the way it is employed in this book and in the feminist argumentation that the book discusses. This point relates to a possible argument suggesting that philosophy is not androcentric. According to this argument (which, I believe, should be rejected), philosophy is not androcentric, since the androcentric claims in it are actually not philosophy. Not everything that a philosopher writes is, of course, philosophy; for example, when she or he writes a shopping list or a thank-you note, she or he is not writing anything philosophical. Similarly, it might be claimed, Kant's suggestions that women should not be considered citizens, or Aristotle's claims that women are less rational than men, are not in fact part of their *philosophy,* and thus do not make their philosophies androcentric. However, I do not think that this is a direction that should be followed. The andro-

17. Midgley and Hughes, *Women's Choices,* 45–46; Midgley, "Sex and Personal Identity," 52.

18. In this I follow Midgley, who although considering whether philosophers' androcentricity could have been avoided in the era when they wrote, was merely bad luck, and so on, argues that "blame is not the point. The interesting question is 'What happens if we now correct that mistake? How much difference will it make to the value of the rest of their thought, and to its bearing on life?'" Midgley, "Sex and Personal Identity," 51.

19. For a different perspective, see Schott, "Gender of Enlightenment," 476.

centric statements that these philosophers present are very similar in all ways, except their theme, to their other statements that are commonly considered as part of their philosophy; and they appear in tracts that are commonly referred to as philosophy, read in philosophy classes, and discussed in what are considered philosophical publications. It seems that it would be too arbitrary, and inconsistent with our uses of "philosophy" and "philosophical" in other cases, to claim that these and similar androcentric statements are not really part of their authors' philosophies.

4

The number of arguments for the androcentricity of philosophy is very large. I have organized them here in several general groups, according to the type of argumentation employed. Chapters 2 through 8 each deal with one general group or type of argument, present several examples of it, and evaluate its strength. The classification of the arguments into types was guided by the effort to emphasize significant characteristics, to include important arguments, to avoid repetition, and to facilitate discussion. Of course, the typology presented here is not the only possible one. An argument can be similar to a second argument in one respect, and to a third argument in another respect, and is thus amenable to being grouped in more than one way. Further, the typology presented here allows for some borderline cases that can be discussed under more than one rubric.

Organizing the discussion by types of arguments precludes other principles of organization. Since the primary division of chapters is according to types of arguments rather than of theories, readers will not find a discussion of the various arguments for the androcentricity of Descartes's theory, and then another of the (largely similar) arguments for the androcentricity of Locke's, and another concerning arguments relating to Kant, and so forth. The same is true of notions. There is no separate chapter dealing with the arguments for the androcentricity of objectivity, and then another on those for the androcentricity of universality, and so on. However, an effort has been made, where possible, to group together discussions of a certain philosopher or a certain notion *within* the different chapters.

Organizing the discussion around general types of arguments also precludes classification by authors of the arguments. Different aspects of, for example, Carol Gilligan's theory are discussed in separate chapters.

Nor are all aspects of each scholar's argument always mentioned, since some of them repeat aspects of other arguments already described. Again, however, where possible, and within chapters, I have tried to follow the work of individual authors.

Chapters 2 through 8 each present several examples of the arguments discussed and evaluated. Of course, only a few examples of each type could be examined in detail. However, what is said of them applies, *mutatis mutandis*, to other arguments of the same type. Several criteria guided the decision regarding which examples to include. An effort was made to present several subtypes of the arguments in question, and to offer, if possible, a fair number of instances of each type. Considerations of interest and theme were also taken into account. And well-cited, influential, and "classical" texts were preferred to lesser-known ones. No effort was made, however, to prefer recent examples to earlier ones. A fair proportion of the arguments presented are from the 1980s and early 1990s, when the case for the androcentricity of philosophy was most forcefully presented, thus establishing views still held today. Moreover, arguments have been included even if they appeared in works whose main topics are not the androcentricity of philosophy, but other themes in philosophy or in feminism, so that claims concerning the androcentricity of philosophy are only noted briefly or implied.

Readers will notice that discussions presented in the book frequently point out more than one difficulty in the arguments critiqued. Since the issues discussed are controversial and hotly debated, I preferred in cases of doubt to err on the side of presenting more rather than less comment than might be strictly necessary. Readers will also notice that many parts of the contentions for the androcentricity of philosophy critiqued here are quoted rather than paraphrased. This may help to elucidate the discussion, which frequently pivots around specific formulations and nuances.

Many authors do not specify whether their arguments purport to show that philosophy is pervasively or nonpervasively androcentric.[20] The discussions ahead examine both possibilities. But it is possible that certain authors who did not specify whether they were discussing pervasive or nonpervasive androcentricity had only the weaker claim in mind. Showing that their arguments fail to sustain the stronger claim may thus

---

20. None use the terms "pervasive androcentricity" or "nonpervasive androcentricity," which are mine; but some do specify whether they think all, or most, or only a small part of the philosophical theory in question should be rejected because of the androcentricity in it.

be arguing against a straw man. Still, I preferred to consider both alternatives.

Chapter 2 deals with arguments based on the explicit androcentric statements that appear in many philosophical theories and proposes that these suffice to make philosophy androcentric. However, it argues that this androcentricity is nonpervasive, and does not call for complete rejection or extensive changes in the systems in which it appears. Chapter 3 deals with arguments that take philosophical theories to be androcentric not because they make any androcentric statements themselves, but because the philosophical notions they include have been associated with androcentric views, stereotypes, or social practices in other contexts. The arguments considered in Chapter 4 do not rely on any openly androcentric philosophical statements either, but contend that many of the notions employed in philosophical theories have harmed women. Chapter 5 discusses arguments for the androcentricity of philosophy based on the appearance of some androcentric metaphors in philosophical theories. It is argued that the arguments appearing in Chapter 5 show philosophy to be nonpervasively androcentric. The arguments appearing in Chapters 3 and 4, however, do not show philosophy to be androcentric in any way.

The same is true for the arguments discussed in Chapters 6 and 7. Chapter 6 examines arguments that stress the differences between women's and men's interests. Such arguments typically claim (or implicitly assume) that women's and men's interests differ, and then contend that philosophy is influenced by, or reflects, men's interests rather than women's. Chapter 7, somewhat similarly, discusses arguments for the androcentricity of philosophy that emphasize cognitive and psychological differences between women and men, and go on to contend that philosophy suits, or reflects, the mentalities of men rather than of women. It is argued that these types of arguments, too, do not suffice to show that philosophy is androcentric in any way.

Chapter 8 discusses a type of argument based on some theories' failure to consider issues relating to women, or to condemn androcentricity. Notwithstanding the somewhat paradoxical nature of such arguments, it is argued that they hold good, and that they too show some philosophies to be androcentric. However, again, it is argued that they show these philosophies to be nonpervasively rather than pervasively androcentric.

The discussion suggests, then, that philosophy is not pervasively androcentric. Yet, based on the view that it is, many efforts have been made to suggest, anticipate, or point to radical alternatives to philosophy. Chapter 9 discusses these efforts and argues that so far they have not been successful. It is maintained that their failure to achieve their end corroborates the claim that philosophy is not pervasively androcentric. Chapter 10 discusses some possible objections to the criticisms and arguments suggested in this book. This consideration includes questions such as whether or not the critique of arguments for the androcentricity of philosophy is circular, since it relies on the very philosophy claimed to be androcentric, or whether arguments for the androcentricity of philosophy would not be stronger if considered together instead of separately, as they are here. The chapter also examines some of the general problems in various arguments for the androcentricity of philosophy, and the place of the discussion in the feminist endeavor at large.

2

Explicit Androcentric Statements

I

The strongest argument for the androcentricity of philosophy is also the
simplest: philosophy is androcentric because many philosophical theories
include explicitly androcentric views. Jean Bethke Elshtain, Arlene W.
Saxonhouse, Susan Moller Okin, Genevieve Lloyd, and Ellen Kennedy
and Susan Mendus, among others, have shown that such androcentric
views are more frequent than many of us would like to believe.[1] Aristotle,
for example, takes wives to be inferior to their husbands; believes that
although women, unlike slaves, do have a deliberative faculty, it is without authority; argues that courage is expressed in men by commanding,
in women by obeying; presents the female as a deviation from, if not a
degenerate version of, the male; and sees the male as the active element
that gives life and furnishes the form of the next generation in reproduc-
tion, while the female is the passive element that provides matter.[2] Locke
believes that when husband and wife disagree about issues of common
concern, "the last determination . . . naturally falls to the man's share as
the abler and the stronger."[3] Rousseau also thinks that women should be

---

1. See Elshtain, *Public Man, Private Woman;* Saxonhouse, *Women in the History of
Political Thought;* Okin, *Women in Western Political Thought;* Lloyd, *Man of Reason;* and
Kennedy and Mendus, *Women in Western Political Philosophy.*

2. See, for example, *Nicomachean Ethics* 1158b13–27 and 1161a23–24; *Politics*
1260a13–14 and 22–23; and *Generation of Animals* 728a16–19, 732a1–11, and
765b10–12.

3. *Two Treatises of Government* II sec. 82.

subjugated to men, and describes women as intellectually inferior.[4] Kant does not believe women can be citizens in the state, and Hegel thinks they should not be involved in political life.[5] Of Schopenhauer's and Nietzsche's views on women little needs to be said. Androcentric views are expressed in many other philosophical theories as well.

These views are clearly very disturbing and show that Western philosophy is indeed androcentric. It remains to be determined, however, whether these androcentric views make philosophy pervasively or nonpervasively androcentric. Do the androcentric passages in these theories make the other views voiced in them, or even the theories as a whole, androcentric? Put differently, does rejecting the androcentric passages in the writings of these philosophers also require rejecting the rest of their teachings (or significant parts of them), or can we still accept all (or almost all) of their nonandrocentric teachings while rejecting their androcentric ones?

Consider the following thought experiment: as we all know, some of Aristotle's works have not survived. Imagine that an esoteric but effective group of medieval monks decided to omit from the writings of Aristotle all the androcentric passages and, having access to all the surviving manuscripts in every monastery, succeeded in doing so. What would we have missed in Aristotle's writings? Could we still make sense of and employ his theories of the four causes, substance, the nature of movement, and his other metaphysical, physical, aesthetic and even most of his moral and political theories? If we could, the androcentric passages do not make the rest of Aristotle's theories and views androcentric, and there is no need to reject, replace, or complement them; the theory is nonpervasively androcentric. If we could not, the androcentric passages do make the rest of Aristotle's philosophy androcentric, and we need to reject, replace, or complement it; the philosophy thus is pervasively androcentric.

Similarly, do the androcentric passages in Kant's political, moral, and anthropological theories make the rest of his teachings androcentric as well? Assume, again as a thought experiment, that the androcentric pas-

---

4. Jean-Jacques Rousseau, *Émile*, in *Jean-Jacques Rousseau: Oeuvres Complètes*, ed. Bernard Gagnebin and Marcel Raymond (Paris: Bibliothèque de la Pléiade, 1969), 4:737, 750.

5. Immanuel Kant, "On the Common Saying: 'This May Be True in Theory, But It Does not Apply in Practice,'" in *Kant's Political Writings,* trans. H. B. Nisbet (Cambridge: Cambridge University Press, 1970), 78; Georg Wilhelm Friedrich Hegel, *Hegel's Philosophy of Right*, trans. T. M. Knox (Oxford: Oxford University Press, 1967), 114.

sages in Kant's writings did not exist at all, or that by some historical accident were erased, or that we were ignorant of them. Could we still make sense of and employ his epistemology, metaphysics, aesthetics, ethics, and the rest of his theories independently of the androcentric passages? If the answer is "yes," there is no need to reject, replace, or reform all or most of the other parts of Kant's philosophy; we can employ most of his theories while rejecting his androcentric views, and his philosophy is nonpervasively androcentric. If the answer is "no," and we could not make sense of and employ his epistemology, metaphysics, aesthetics, ethics, and so on without the androcentric passages, then his philosophy is pervasively androcentric.

I will argue here that the androcentric statements that appear in philosophies make them only nonpervasively androcentric. There is no logical necessity here; in principle, the androcentric statements *could* make the systems pervasively androcentric. However, various conditions that need to be fulfilled for this to happen are realized in no philosophy I can think of. One such condition is that all or most of the philosophy in question discuss in an androcentric way women, men, or the relation between them. Thus, rejecting or reforming the androcentric claims would amount to rejecting or reforming most or all of what constitutes that philosophy, and it would be pervasively androcentric. Yet none of the philosophies I am familiar with discuss—androcentrically or otherwise—men, women, or the relation between them elaborately and extensively. The typical interests or subject matter of philosophical theories are different, and they usually dedicate relatively very little place to presenting androcentric statements. This is true even for famously androcentric philosophers such as Schopenhauer or Nietzsche. Since little of the discussion in philosophical theories consists of androcentric assertions about women and men, then, rejecting or reforming those assertions transforms only a small part of the theory.

Failing to fulfill the first condition, androcentric statements can still render a philosophy pervasively androcentric if they are tied to (sufficiently many) other, nonandrocentric statements so that rejecting the androcentric statements requires rejecting the other, nonandrocentric ones as well. However, as Jean Grimshaw points out, "One cannot simply *assume* that the opinions philosophers hold about women affect or are integral to the rest of their philosophical work."[6] As I will argue ahead, in all or almost all cases the androcentric statements are not linked to

---

6. *Philosophy and Feminist Thinking*, 37; Grimshaw's emphasis.

other theses so that rejecting the former requires rejecting the latter. The androcentric and nonandrocentric theses simply coexist in the same writings. Thus, in all or almost all cases the androcentric opinions are in fact not integral to the rest of the philosophical work, and the second condition is rarely, if ever, fulfilled.

It may be answered that the presupposition assumed in the claims and thought experiments suggested earlier, namely, that some parts of philosophical theories may be accepted while others are rejected, is wrong. Susan Mendus has argued that "philosophical systems are *systems* precisely because their various parts fit together, and for that reason it may well be difficult to isolate individual themes and declare them superfluous to the system as a whole."[7] However, this is frequently not the case. It is easier to see this in analytic philosophy, where many authors openly present themselves more as puzzle solvers than as system builders, and explicitly assert that they do not aspire to suggest closely knit, cohesive theories. It is more difficult to see this in some traditional Continental philosophies that have been presented by their authors or interpreters as systems made of strongly interrelated theses. Yet even these theories are almost always less cohesive than they may at first appear. Whereas some theses are interconnected with many others, some are not. In Kant, for example, dismissing the distinction between phenomena and noumena would affect much in his ontology, epistemology, and ethics, while discarding, say, his view on the importance of practice for efficient learning, expressed in his philosophy of education, would not.[8] Indeed, we frequently accept one view, or a set of views, of a certain philosopher, without agreeing with all others. It seems, then, that although the teachings of many philosophers are frequently represented as systems, they are almost always less cohesive than they may at first appear.

Theses in a philosophy may be necessary conditions for other theses; may be sufficient conditions for other theses; may be merely consistent with other theses; or may contradict other theses. Rejecting a thesis requires rejecting others only when the former is a necessary condition to the others. When a thesis is merely a sufficient condition for others, is merely consistent with them, or contradicts them, rejecting it does not require rejecting them as well. At first it may be surprising to note how, in most theories, including those presented as systems, most theses are

---

7. "How Androcentric Is Western Philosophy?" 63; Mendus's emphasis.

8. Immanuel Kant, *Pädagogik*, in *Kant's Gesammelte Schriften*, Academy Edition (Berlin and Leipzig: Walter de Gruyter, 1923), 9:477.

not necessary conditions for others (and hence most theses are also not sufficient conditions for others, since if A is a necessary condition for B, B is a sufficient condition for A). Most theses, in most systems, are simply consistent with other theses. Examining androcentric theses shows that they, too, either contradict the other, nonandrocentric theses, or are merely consistent with them. It is difficult to find cases where androcentric theses are sufficient conditions for nonandrocentric theses, and even harder to find cases where androcentric theses are necessary conditions for nonandrocentric ones. Since neither the first nor the second of the two conditions mentioned earlier (that most statements in a given philosophy would be androcentric, or, if there are only a few androcentric statements, that they would be tied to sufficiently many other statements in the philosophy) is fulfilled in Western philosophies, androcentric statements in philosophical systems do not make them pervasively androcentric.

Various philosophical analyses, however, represent (or are frequently read as representing) some systems, or political philosophies, as pervasively androcentric. In what follows I will consider four such discussions, and attempt to show that, on closer scrutiny, the teachings considered are not pervasively androcentric.

2

An important source for the argument that some philosophical theories are rendered androcentric by the explicit androcentric opinions they include is Susan Moller Okin's *Women in Western Political Thought*. It is not always easy to determine whether she takes the philosophies she discusses to be pervasively androcentric. However, expressions such as "the works of our philosophical heritage are to *a very great extent built on the assumption of the inequality of the sexes*"[9] do suggest that Okin sees the philosophies she discusses as pervasively androcentric, and she is frequently read as making such a claim. I examine her discussion of the androcentricity in Aristotle and Rousseau as if it indeed aims to show that their political-moral theories are pervasively androcentric.[10]

Can Aristotle's androcentric claims about women be rejected without

9. *Women in Western Political Thought*, 10; my emphasis.
10. If this is an incorrect reading of Okin, and she takes these theories to be only nonpervasively androcentric, my discussion ahead will show that the theories are significantly less androcentric than Okin takes them to be.

rejecting at the same time other parts of his philosophy? Okin points out that Aristotle's androcentric views are related to various general basic assumptions, and rejecting the androcentric views would require reject-ing the basic assumptions as well. Rejecting these basic assumptions, however, is no small matter, since it would lead also to the rejection of many nonandrocentric views that are deduced from the assumptions. Okin argues, for example, that "Aristotle's identification of the hierarchi-cal status quo with the natural, the necessary, and the good, cannot with-stand the emancipation of women into political life" (277). Thus, if women were to be emancipated, this identification, and all that relies on it, would be undermined.

Aristotle, however, does not always identify the good, the natural, and the necessary with the status quo; hence, the egalitarian exception to the status quo does not unsettle his system in the way it may at first seem to. For example, Aristotle devotes almost the entire tenth book of his *Nicomachean Ethics* to recommending the ideal of the contemplative life, although this practice was hardly typical of the citizens of the Greek city of his time. Furthermore, he presents as the object of the contemplative life the Unmoved Mover, which is more akin to a monotheistic God than to conventional Greek deities, and uncharacteristic of the religious prac-tice of a Greek city of his time. Again, contrary to the conventions of his time, he characterizes pederasty as morbid (1148b25–30). And as Arlene Saxonhouse shows, his political programs were similarly out of step. For example, in book 7 of the *Politics,* he openly presents the characteristics of the ideal city and the way it should be run as an ideal, and hardly relies on accepted conventions and norms.[11] Likewise, again as Saxon-house shows, in book 4 of the *Politics* Aristotle discusses various kinds of constitutions and explains why the one he thinks is likely to be generally beneficial—based on the "middle sort" of citizens—is the one that is his-torically rare (1295b34–1296b11).

Nor does Aristotle always identify the status quo with nature, as can be seen in his discussion of slavery, where he distinguishes between slaves by convention, on the one hand, and slaves by nature, on the other (1255a3–b15). Furthermore, as Saxonhouse shows, he asserts that the actual cities of his time deviate from the natural order.[12] Okin herself notes that in general "his use of the word *physis* (nature) and its deriva-tives is at least as complex and ambiguous as Plato's."[13]

11. Saxonhouse, *Women in the History of Political Thought,* 88–90.
12. Ibid., 69–71, 74–80.
13. *Women in Western Political Thought,* 79.

Aristotle's moral and political views, then, can diverge from commonly accepted views or the status quo. Accepted convention is important for him, but is not the only moral consideration he takes into account. It is frequently the starting point of his discussion, not its end. Nor is it his only starting point; the views of his philosophical predecessors, even when they were not commonly accepted, constitute a similarly important beginning. His discussion frequently goes beyond these starting points, testifying to his readiness to diverge from common views.

It may be answered that my suggestion about the place of the status quo, or the accepted views, in Aristotle's theory is proven false by his assertion that

> we must, as in all other cases, set the observed facts before us and, after first discussing the difficulties, go on to prove, if possible, the truth of all the common opinions about these affections of the mind, or, failing this, of the greater number and the most authoritative; for if we both refute the objections and leave the common opinions undisturbed, we shall have proved the case sufficiently. (*Politics* 1145b1–7; cited in Okin, *Women in Western Political Thought*, 73–74)

Okin argues, in relation to this passage, that "[Aristotle] perceives his task as moral philosopher, then, as that of redeeming prevailing moral views and standards from whatever inconsistencies or vagueness might mar them. The assumption is that they are far more likely to be right than wrong" (74). However, Aristotle is not claiming in this passage that the task of a moral philosopher is merely to redeem prevailing moral views from inconsistencies (although he does believe that prevailing moral views are more likely to be right than wrong). He is suggesting that prevailing views are an important but not an exclusive consideration; observable facts should also be taken into account, and objections or contradictions should be discussed and resolved. Aristotle's methodology, then, is looser and more pluralistic than it may initially seem, and it allows the use of different methods, singly and in combination, to reach a conclusion. Hence, changing, or rejecting, Aristotle's androcentric views does not require changing or rejecting an entire methodological foundation of his moral-political thinking and the moral and political teachings based upon it.

Rejecting Aristotle's androcentricity may seem to undermine the whole political system also because it would conflict with another basic presupposition, that of inequality. Okin suggests that Aristotle's "system of politics is so extensively based on inequalities that to deny any aspect of the inequality jeopardizes the entire structure" (277). As before, however, although Aristotle's political thought does presuppose a certain measure of inequality, it does not exclude every form of equality. He does not call for a state in which all individuals, or all conceivable groups of individuals, would be treated as unequal. Those aged thirty, for example, do not have different rights than those aged fifty, and those inclined toward poetry do not have different rights than those inclined toward athletics. He calls, then, for partial rather than complete inequality, and denying inequality between two specific groups, for example, women and men, does not jeopardize his entire political structure.[14]

Rejecting the androcentric passages in Aristotle's moral and political writings has to be accompanied, of course, by a rejection of the biological androcentric passages, such as those claiming that the females of the species are deformities; or that the male is the form while the female is only the matter; or that in fertilization the male supplies the form of the embryo and the female the matter.[15] It might be argued that rejecting all this would require too many changes in Aristotelian theory, since some of Aristotle's biological views are entailed by his ontological principles. For example, it might be argued, rejecting Aristotle's view that in fertilization the male supplies the form of the embryo, while the female the matter, would require also rejecting his ontological principle that the form is the active element, matter the passive one. However, rejecting the notion that the male supplies the form of the embryo, the female the matter, does not also require rejecting the view that form is the active element. It may be contended, instead, that both parents supply the form of the embryo, or that the male supplies the form of the offspring in half of the cases, and the female in the other half. Hypothesizing this would even solve a difficulty in Aristotle's theory as it stands now, namely, that the male, who supposedly is the source of the offspring, in about half the cases creates a *female* baby, namely, matter.[16] There is also the difficulty of explaining

14. Okin also discusses the teleological functionalist supposition in Aristotle (ibid., 276–77). However, the discussion is combined with a discussion of the "status quo presupposition" and the "inequality presupposition," which I have already dealt with. The Aristotelian teleological presupposition, namely, that all things have an end, which is their actuality, and so on, would not in itself be undermined if women's and men's ends were seen as similar.

15. See, for example, *Generation of Animals* 728a16–19, 732a1–11, and 765b10–12.

16. For Aristotle's elaborate efforts to cope with this problem, see ibid., 765a24–767a35 and 767b7–768a11.

how, if the male furnishes the embryo's form while the female only the matter, the physical as well as mental characteristics of the offspring are sometimes similar to those of the mother, or the mother's family.[17] Hypothesizing that sometimes the male furnishes the form and sometimes the female, and sometimes both to varying degrees, would correspond better with the empiricist tendency of Aristotle's philosophy. Like his political and ethical teachings, Aristotle's biological theory is sufficiently composite and flexible, and in some cases sufficiently unclear, contradictory, and hospitable to inexplicable phenomena, to accommodate equality between the sexes without undermining its basic principles. In some cases, moreover, hypothesizing equality rather than male superiority even helps solve problems in the theory.

As Okin correctly points out, some other changes would have to be introduced into Aristotle's theory if women were to be hypothesized as equal to men. The family could no longer be considered an object of property, and would need to be considered "an institution initiated and supported by its adult members as complete equals" (*Women in Western Political Thought*, 276). Some new arrangements for the management of the household would have to be made, and the family would have to be defined within the realm of the political (275–76). However, viewing women as completely equal to men does not require that the family cease being considered an object of property; it could continue to be considered as such, but would now belong to both husband and wife. Moreover, Aristotle already defines the family within the realm of the political (*Politics* 1252b9ff.). The arrangements for the management of the household could consist in the equal division of all household activities between husband and wife, and perhaps some additional changes in the understanding of some aspects of the family would have to be introduced, but this does not necessitate any changes in it except those involving, again, the equality between husband and wife, and some laws that guarantee equality within the family.[18]

Thus, rejecting all the androcentric claims in Aristotle's theory will

17. For Aristotle's efforts to cope with this problem, see ibid., 767a35–768b35.

18. I expect that most readers would also wish to reject some other claims in Aristotle's theory, for example, those concerning slaves and artisans. They can do so by committing themselves to further, but still not major, changes. For example, if slavery ceases to exist and artisans are considered equal to other citizens, some of the inhabitants of the city will have to live less luxurious lives than they previously had, work more, and devote somewhat less time to the contemplative life or to public civil affairs. And others, of course, could live better, work less, and devote some time to public civil affairs and the contemplative life. But most of Aristotle's ethics and politics could still remain the same.

not jeopardize it. Almost all of the moral-political views can remain as they are. One can still accept, if one so wishes, Aristotle's views on the right type of constitution, the contemplative life, and civil participation; the wrongfulness of excessive wealth and especially of usury; friendship; incontinence; the middle way; and the moral syllogism. Aristotle's political-moral theory, as well as his theory at large, then, exhibit nonpervasive rather than pervasive androcentricity.[19]

3

Judith M. Green presents another argument suggesting that the androcentricity in Aristotle's philosophy is pervasive.[20] Green suggests that "Aristotle's remarks about women and slaves are conclusions of a consistent and coherent theoretical corpus, so that the theoretical first principles and general philosophical methodology on which they are based must be regarded as unreliable" (71). Moreover, "for Aristotle 'the masculine' and 'the feminine' are principle-bundles of complementary oppositions in all of Nature, the most fundamental value-creating differences from which other value-creating differences arise" (ibid.). These claims are based on passages in the *Physics* from which Green deduces that, for Aristotle

19. While examining which nonandrocentric claims would need to be changed if the androcentric claims are rejected, I have followed Okin's presentation. It should be noted, however, that there are other important and interesting accounts of Aristotle's androcentricity. Arlene Saxonhouse argues that "Aristotle's understanding of the female in the political world leads to a vision of hierarchy, but not submission on all levels." *Women in the History of Political Thought*, 90. She sees Aristotle's views of women as complex. For example, although Aristotle does think that women are by nature inferior to men, he also thinks that there are many cases where nature does not fulfill itself, and in these, women may be superior to men. Thus, although men are superior to women by nature, not all men are better than all women in fact (69–72). Moreover, Aristotle notes that men are rendered superior to women also by convention, but as in his discussion of slaves, he thinks that convention can be problematic (70–71). Although Aristotle does cite Sophocles's line, "Silence brings orderliness to a woman," Sophocles gives these words to Ajax when he is half mad, is behaving wrongly, and should clearly follow the sober and wise view of his wife, Tecmessa (73). Nor does Aristotle say, according to Saxonhouse's translation, that men are superior to women, but that they have authority over women, which may or may not be justified (74). Saxonhouse's other comments also present Aristotle's philosophy as less androcentric, and treat the androcentricity as more complex, than it at first glance seems to be.

20. Green, "Aristotle on Necessary Verticality," 70–96.

the general principles of Nature . . . concern the systematic inter-action of dualistic oppositions, such as activity and passivity, up-ness and down-ness, heat and cold, form-making and form-re-ceiving. According to the *Physics,* these dualistic oppositions are systematically organized into principle-bundles; that is, activity tends to go with up-ness, heat and form-making among natural things that have any one of these characteristics, whereas passiv-ity tends to go with down-ness, cold, and form receiving (188a26ff. and 190b29ff.). (74)

Moreover, in *Generation of Animals* Aristotle maintains that the male is hot, active, form-making, and dominant (729a5–35; Green, "Aristotle on Necessary Verticality," 82). From this Green concludes that

though there seems to be no place in his extant works in which Aristotle explicitly names the opposite dualistic principle-bun-dles "the masculine principles" and "the feminine principles," these passages in *De Generatione Animalium*, read against the background of the earlier works, suggest that ascription of gen-der to the principle-bundles themselves is what he has in mind. If one takes this ascription of gender to his principle-bundles se-riously, a whole new order within Aristotle's scientific and politi-cal vision is revealed. It suggests that Aristotle, like some of his radical feminist critics, regards the masculine/feminine dichot-omy as the fundamental characteristic of all dualisms. (82)

I would like to suggest, however, that this is a problematic reading of Aristotle's philosophy. In *Physics* 188a26ff. Aristotle does say that "they [previous thinkers] all in one way or another identify the contraries with the principles. And with good reason."[21] But although he finds some vir-tue in his predecessors' views (as he frequently does), he does not commit himself to them. Moreover, Aristotle does not discuss in that passage any of the dualistic oppositions mentioned by Green, and he relates the discussion to the question of the number of the basic elements of nature, remaining undecided whether there are two or three (189b29). In 190b29ff. Aristotle adduces only one of the dualistic oppositions men-tioned by Green, hot and cold, along with the musical and the unmusical,

---

21. The translation follows the revised Oxford translation of *The Complete Works of Aristotle,* ed. Jonathan Barnes (Princeton: Princeton University Press, 1984), 1:321.

and the tuned and the untuned, distinguishing there between substrate (for example, man) and opposites (for example, musical or unmusical). In 208b19–22 Aristotle does write that fire and what is light are carried up, and what is made of earth and is weighty are carried down, and in 211a4–5 that all bodies are carried to their proper places and rest there, and this makes the places either "up" or "down." But this is insufficient to corroborate the claim that up-ness and down-ness belong to dualistic principle-bundles that are the general principles of nature. Nor is the assertion that the "principle-bundles" should be identified as the "masculine" or "feminine" sufficiently corroborated. It should be noted, moreover, that Aristotle does not employ in any of his explanations and theories what, according to the interpretation discussed here, are his "general principles of nature."

4

Rousseau's philosophy also includes explicit androcentric views. Okin writes that if the hypothesis of women's and men's equality were inserted into Rousseau's philosophy, women's education into submissiveness would have to be changed, and Émile's and Sophie's educations would have to be similar. Moreover, women's character and way of life would not be defined in terms of men's needs, or no more than men's character and way of life are defined in terms of women's (*Women in Western Political Thought,* 278). Rousseau's "great fear of dependency, except on a person one can control," would have to be censured (ibid.), and the possibility of a trusting relationship between wives and husbands would also have to be recognized (ibid.). Okin also believes that "the *entire* structure of the family would have to be radically altered, so as to be consistent with the equal rights and responsibilities of its adult members" (ibid.; my emphasis). She adds that

> women . . . , too, would have to spend a considerable amount of time in political meetings and other public activities. But Rousseau's republic is based on the institutions of the family, private property, and inheritance, and both private families and private holdings require a considerable amount of individual nurturance. While Rousseau says that the formal education of citizens is to be public, it is clear that he conceives of the early child-

rearing as a private activity, and sees the household as a place of refuge, for the man, from the tiring demands of the world outside. If all the adults of both sexes were to be as much preoccupied with civic activity as citizenship in a direct democracy requires, who would maintain this private sphere of life which Rousseau perceives as crucially important? It is clear that considerable inroads would need to be made into the privacy and exclusiveness of the family, in order to allow women to participate fully as citizens.

Thus it would appear that, at least in an egalitarian society, one cannot achieve both the great intensity of civic life and the wholly private realm of family life without dichotomizing the spheres of operations of the sexes. (278–79)

It seems to me that the changes required are more limited. The household would not be a place of complete refuge, for men, from the demands of the world outside; rather, it would be a partial refuge for both men and women, as well as a place of certain household and private demands. The intensive involvement of citizens in the direct democracy may have to be somewhat lessened, but need not be so; since many more citizens (namely, women) would share the burden, the required involvement may stay more or less the same. The institutions of private property and inheritance need not change much, except that they would belong to both genders, and would pass through the generations, in an egalitarian way. The required changes, then, are more local and limited than suggested.

While these modifications would require some changes, many of Rousseau's views need not change at all if the androcentric views are omitted from his theory: all his nonandrocentric views about education, the social contract, the theory of the general will and freedom, the evil in civilization, the origin of inequality, the two types of self-love, and the source of inauthenticity and many specific details concerning the affairs of state could remain intact. Moreover, as Okin notes, omitting Rousseau's androcentric views would solve some inconsistencies in the theory, such as that between what he says about the servility of women to men on the one hand and his bold assertions about freedom and equality on the other (277). Inserting the hypothesis of men and women's equality into Rousseau's philosophy, then, does not significantly affect the theory. Rousseau's philosophy, too, is only nonpervasively androcentric.

5

Kant—who according to Barbara Herman has the "unhappy status as the modern moral philosopher feminists find most objectionable"—presents contradicting claims concerning women.[22] On the one hand, in his *Theory and Practice*, he writes that in order to be regarded as a citizen (that is, a voting member of the commonwealth), a person should be an adult, have some property, be economically his own master, and be male.[23] This view is by and large repeated in *The Metaphysics of Morals,* where Kant, employing a somewhat different terminology, writes that although they are citizens, women—like men whose existence depends on that of others, for example, apprentices and servants—should be considered nonactive citizens and denied voting rights. Since they lack sufficient independence, their votes may simply reflect the views of those on whom they depend. However, while in *Theory and Practice* Kant does not suggest that his criteria for citizenship are in any way flexible, or that those who do not fit them may somehow, even if in the distant future, become citizens, he does write in *The Metaphysics of Morals* that laws should be organized so that all those who have only passive citizenship would have the possibility to develop into active citizenship.[24]

Such contradictions also beset Kant's other claims about women. As Robert B. Louden shows, Kant's works include many passages suggesting that he does not see women as members of the moral community and many other passages suggesting that he does.[25] On the one hand, Kant "hardly believes the fair sex is capable of principles."[26] But on the other hand, he is "logically committed to the belief that the entire human species must eventually share in the destiny of the species: moral perfection" (Louden, *Kant's Impure Ethics*, 105). For example, Kant thinks that "with women feelings of honor must take the place of principles."[27] And for him, honor—unlike principles—is related to inclination rather than reason, and is not autonomous. This, together with other arguments cited by Louden and others, suggests that Kant thinks that women are

22. Herman, "Kant on Sex and Marriage," 50.

23. Kant, "On the Common Saying," 78.

24. Kant, The Doctrine of Right, *The Metaphysics of Morals,* trans. Mary Gregor (Cambridge: Cambridge University Press, 1996), sec. 46.

25. *Kant's Impure Ethics,* 82–87, 101–6.

26. *Beobachtungen über das Gefühl des Schönen und Erhabenen,* Academy Edition, 2:232, translated and cited in Louden, *Kant's Impure Ethics,* 105.

27. *Menschenkunde,* Academy Edition, 25:1170, translated and cited in Louden, *Kant's Impure Ethics,* 86.

not, and can never become, rational beings and part of the moral community. However, as Louden points out, Kant also repeatedly declares that the *whole* human race progresses toward moral perfection (101–6). Moreover, as Louden shows, Kant declares in the first paragraph of "The Character of the Sexes" that both men and women are rational beings (84). And as Igor Primoratz pointed out to me, Kant argues in *The Metaphysics of Morals* that polygamy, prostitution, concubinage, and morganatic marriage are wrong since they reduce women to the status of *things*.[28] But for Kant things/persons is an exhaustive and exclusive dichotomy. Thus, condemning polygamy, prostitution, and so on for reducing women to the status of things shows that he regularly considers women to be persons, that is, in his theory, as rational beings and part of the moral community. Similarly, Kant opposes sexual activity outside marriage, arguing that it reduces both women and men to the status of things (sec. 25). This too shows that he does not see women as things but as rational, moral agents. Kant also writes that the right of both sexes to marriage arises from "one's duty to oneself, that is, to the humanity in one's own person."[29] But the term "duty," employed here with reference to both women and men (as also in the same section, in the discussion of both parents' duties to their offspring), again shows that Kant takes women to be moral agents, since in his moral theory only rational, autonomous agents have duties.

It is thus probably impossible to present a noncontradictory interpretation of Kant's view on women's rationality and morality. I believe that Susan Mendus's discussion of Kant does not give sufficient weight to these contradictions in his views. Mendus concludes that in Kant's moral-political philosophy "it is denied—fleetingly and indirectly, but nevertheless denied—that women's nature has a connection with reason. . . . It would appear that in the kingdom of rational beings there are only adult males."[30] She also suggests that in Kant's treatment of women "there are no tensions at all: there is no radicalism or idealism to set against the pragmatism and conservatism" (384). But this seems not to give sufficient weight to the many passages where Kant asserts or presupposes that women are rational, moral beings, as well as to his many assertions about the progress of the *whole* human race toward perfection.

Similarly, Mendus argues that

28. Igor Primoratz, private conversation, September 2000; Kant, "The Doctrine of Right," in *The Metaphysics of Morals*, sec. 26.

29. Sec. 28, in *The Metaphysics of Morals*.

30. "Kant," 380–81.

> summarizing, we may present Kant's views about women's status as follows. Woman may be accorded the status of passive citizen only. Unlike male passive citizens, she may not, by self-improvement or advancement, aspire to the status of active citizen. This is because of her intrinsic nature as exemplified in the marriage contract. (380–81)

Mendus adds that "woman is denied not only the vote but also all hope of aspiring to it. Independence is eternally withheld from her" (382). But this too seems not to give sufficient weight to Kant's proposition in the *Metaphysics of Morals*, that *all* those with only passive citizenship should have the possibility to develop into active citizenship, and, again, to Kant's many other assertions about the progress of the whole human race toward perfection.[31]

Mendus also takes Kant's view about wives' subjection to their husbands to relate to a central tenet in his philosophy: his individualism. She argues that "the problem here is a deep one—not only for Kant, but for individualism generally" (385). "All individualist theories share this difficulty: in construing persons as essentially independent, free and equal, they support an atomistic model which cannot readily accommodate those social units, such as the family, which transcend mere atomism" (ibid). Relying on the work of Elizabeth Wolgast, Mendus suggests that seeing the family as a unit conflicts with seeing its members as individuals. In order to solve this problem, it is easier to take one of the individuals (frequently the husband) as representing all other members and the family as a whole. Thus, individualism "dictates, as a central tenet, that *someone* must dominate, *someone* must give way" (386; Mendus's emphases). This is true also of individualist feminism, which can only aspire that, in some of the cases, women rather the men will be those who dominate, but "is never in doubt that *someone* must be the head and decision-maker. The language of domination and subordination is central to individualism and cannot be dispended with except by abandoning individualism itself" (ibid.; Mendus's emphasis).

Individualism is indeed central to Kant's philosophy, and rejecting it from the theory will require also many other changes. However, androcentricity and individualism are not cohesively linked in Kant's theory, and one may reject the former without rejecting the latter. Kant's individualism need not lead to androcentricity or other types of inequality (nor

---

31. Mendus mentions these passages herself (see "Kant," 372–74).

must individualism lead to androcentricity or other types of inequality in general or in other philosophical systems). Individuals in families can retain their individuality yet reach, through discussion and negotiation, joint decisions to which they contribute equally and which do justice to the interests and wishes of all. Such decisions can be seen as reflecting the family unit as a whole. Notwithstanding its individualism, then, Kant's theory need not be androcentric, and one can reject the androcentric elements from the theory without rejecting its individualism or other central tenets. Kant's theory emerges as merely nonpervasively androcentric.[32]

6

I have presented here four examples where philosophies that might seem, because of the androcentric statements in them, to be pervasively androcentric are, in fact, not so. It might be answered that these are only four examples, and other discussions, of these and other philosophies, may yet prove them to be pervasively androcentric. I agree that this is possible, although I have not yet found such cases. The considerations presented in section 1 of this chapter explain why it is unlikely that these or other philosophies would be made pervasively androcentric by the androcentric statements they include. But I can only invite the reader to examine for herself or himself other philosophies that include such statements.

Feminist philosophy should be commended for pointing out the presence of androcentric theses in philosophical theories. Their existence should be acknowledged, not ignored. But, of course, their place in these philosophies should not be exaggerated. To say, for example, that Aristotle's philosophy is pervasively androcentric because of certain passages is as valid as to say that his and other philosophies are pervasively theological because of the theological passages they include, or pervasively aesthetic because of the aesthetic passages. The works of Aristotle, Plato, Kant, and many others are theological to some extent and aesthetic to some extent, but not pervasively so (unlike, for example, Karl Barth's, or George Dickey's). They are also secular, biological, anthropological, pedagogical, and—since they also contain nonandrocentric passages—nonandrocentric. Notwithstanding some androcentric views, which should indeed be rejected, most of Western philosophy can—at least in this respect—be accepted as it is.

32. For another discussion that, I believe, does not give due attention to Kant's nonandrocentric statements on women, see Schott, "Gender of Enlightenment."

3

Associations, Stereotypes, and Social Practices

I

Another group of arguments for the androcentricity of philosophy takes philosophy, or a philosophy, to be androcentric, not because it says anything explicitly androcentric (such cases were discussed in the previous chapter), but because it says something—usually, presents a preference for a category—that has been linked with explicitly androcentric stereotypes or social practices in *other* contexts. Many of these arguments focus on—indeed, oppose—philosophical or cultural dualisms. However, their essential and problematic feature is their inference from androcentricity in one context to androcentricity in another. It is on this feature that I aim to concentrate in my critique. An example may help to clarify this.

One of the most frequently cited and influential texts to argue in this fashion is Genevieve Lloyd's *The Man of Reason.* In this book Lloyd discusses many philosophers, and many of her arguments point to explicit androcentric remarks that make the philosophies in which they appear androcentric. Some other arguments deal with androcentric metaphors. There is no need to discuss such arguments here, since explicit androcentric remarks were discussed in the previous chapter, and androcentric metaphors will be discussed in Chapter 5. I focus here on another argument of Lloyd's, in her discussion of Descartes. Descartes makes no explicit androcentric statements; if his philosophy is androcentric, it is so for another reason. Lloyd, too, is very clear on the egalitarian aspects of Descartes's philosophizing (*Man of Reason*, 44–45, 48), but her discussion points at other issues in his theory. One concerns his mind-body distinction. While some of Descartes's predecessors include in the soul both higher (rational) and lower (sensuous or irrational) elements, Descartes includes in the soul only the higher elements, and identifies the nonrational elements with the body. Thus, in Descartes, reason should dominate, or dissociate itself, not from other parts of the intellect, but from the body (46). In connection with this distinction between mind and body, Descartes also distinguishes sharply between theoretical inquiry into truth and practical concerns (46–47). Because of this, however,

> Reason took on special associations with the realm of pure thought, which provides the foundations of science, and with the deductive ratiocination which was of the essence of his method. And the sharpness of his separation of the ultimate requirements of truth-seeking from the practical affairs of everyday life reinforced already existing distinctions between male and female roles, opening the way to the idea of distinctive male and female consciousness.
>
> We owe to Descartes an influential and pervasive theory of mind, which provides support for a powerful version of the sexual division of mental labour. Women have been assigned responsibility for that realm of the sensuous which the Cartesian Man of Reason must transcend, if he is to have true knowledge of things. . . . The way was thus opened for women to be associated with not just a lesser presence of Reason, but a different kind of intellectual character, construed as complementary to "male" Reason. (49–50)

Descartes's philosophy, then, is taken here to be androcentric not because it makes any androcentric claims but because it favors categories (for example, mind, theory) that have been associated with men in *other* contexts, or because it merely suggests the disfavoring of categories (for example, body, "the practical affairs of everyday life") that have been identified with women in other contexts. In this way, Cartesianism is taken to have contributed to, or influenced, the harm inflicted on women.[1] Similar ar-

---

1. Lloyd later interprets *The Man of Reason* as centrally concerned with *metaphors* rather than with associations. "Maleness, Metaphor, and the 'Crisis' of Reason," 71. However, this is a problematic interpretation of her discussions of Descartes and some other philosophers in *The Man of Reason*, which do not even mention metaphors. Elsewhere she makes a weaker claim, writing that "if I were *now* to articulate the central claims of the

guments appear in other discussions.[2] The argument can be presented thus:

1. A philosophy presents a preference for a certain nonandrocentric category, without in any way linking it androcentrically with women or men (or femininity, masculinity, and so on), or using it in any other androcentric way.
2. Other contexts do androcentrically link the category in question with women or men (or femininity, masculinity, and so on).
3. Conclusion: The philosophy in question involves male discrimination against women, leads to the domination of women by men, and so on; that is, the philosophy in question is androcentric.

A somewhat different version of this argument proceeds from the social reality of women's lives. Nancy Tuana, for example, notes that Descartes calls on us to be rational. Moreover, he believes that both women and men can and should be equally rational.[3] However, women have less time than men, as well as less freedom from chores and occupations, to carry out rational activities (40–41). Somewhat similar arguments appear in other discussions.[4] The argument can be presented thus:

1. A philosophy presents a preference for a nonandrocentric activity, without in any way linking it androcentrically with women or men (or femininity, masculinity, and so on), or using it in any other androcentric way.
2. Because the social reality is androcentric, and excludes women from various spheres and activities, women have a lesser (or no) chance, in that androcentric social reality, to successfully engage in that recommended activity.
3. Conclusion: The philosophy in question suits men's experiences or

---

book, I would give much more prominence to metaphorical aspects of the male-female distinction" Preface to the second edition of *The Man of Reason*, viii; my emphasis.

2. See, for example, Thompson, "Women and the High Priests of Reason," 12, where she discusses in a similar way the Cartesian distinction "between *real* knowledge belonging to the 'grand' disciplines and the knowledge required for everyday life" (Thompson's emphasis).

3. Tuana, *Woman and the History of Philosophy*, 39.

4. Thompson, for example, points out that one needs dedication, education, and time in order to achieve Cartesian rationality. However, this is "something that is beyond the means of more women than men." "Women and the High Priests of Reason," 12. See also Lloyd, *Man of Reason*, 48–49.

minds more than women's, or involves male discrimination against women, or leads to the domination of women by men; that is, the philosophy in question is androcentric.

Yet another version of the argument focuses on stereotypes and self-images. Thompson, for example, argues that the dedication, education, and time necessary in order to reason in the Cartesian way are popularly considered, by both men and women, to be irreconcilable with women's occupations and responsibilities ("Women and the High Priests of Reason," 12). Further, Cartesian reason is supposed to be objective and concerned with universals rather than particular issues, and to ignore the seductions of the body. However, according to some stereotypes, women are more related to bodily seductions than men, and are less objective and concerned with universals (12). More generally, Descartes sharpens the distinction between rational knowledge and sensuous belief, and hence also between "what is spiritual, objective, untainted, masculine, and the earthy, impure, pragmatic realm which women are supposed to be bound to" (13). Somewhat similar arguments appear also in other discussions.[5] This version of the argument can be presented thus:

1. A philosophy presents a preference for a nonandrocentric category or activity, without in any way linking it androcentrically with women or men (or femininity, masculinity, and so on), or using it in any other androcentric way.

2. Various androcentric stereotypes or social images suggest that women are less attuned to, or suitable for, the category or activity in question.

3. Because of these stereotypes and social images, women have a lesser chance of successfully engaging in the recommended category or activity.

4. Conclusion: The philosophy in question suits men's experiences or minds more than women's, or involves male discrimination against women, or leads to the domination of women by men; that is, the philosophy in question is androcentric.

In many cases, such arguments relate not to this or that individual philosophy but to philosophy at large. Lloyd, for example, employs them (among other types of arguments) to claim that

5. Tuana, for example, adds to previous accounts that Cartesianism encourages us to be intellectually active. However, women have traditionally been associated with passivity. *Woman and the History of Philosophy*, 41.

it is clear that what we have in the history of philosophical thought is no mere succession of surface misogynist attitudes, which can now be shed, while leaving intact the deeper structures of our ideals of Reason. There is more at stake than the fact that past philosophers believed there to be flaws in female character. . . . Within the context of this association of maleness with preferred traits, it is not just incidental to the feminine that female traits have been construed as inferior—or, more subtly, as "complementary"—to male norms of human excellence. Rationality has been conceived as transcendence of the feminine; and the "feminine" itself has been partly constituted by its occurrence within this structure. (*Man of Reason,* 103–4)

Moreover,

notwithstanding many philosophers' hopes and aspirations to the contrary, our ideals of Reason are in fact male; and if there is a Reason genuinely common to all, it is something to be achieved in the future, not celebrated in the present. Past ideals of Reason, far from transcending sexual difference, have helped to constitute it. That ideas of maleness have developed under the guise of supposedly neutral ideals of Reason has been to the disadvantage of women and men alike. (107–8)

Such arguments, frequently influenced by Lloyd's work, abound.[6] If they are accepted, they show many philosophies to be pervasively androcentric, since the notions they condemn as androcentric, such as having a preference for reason, or mind, are central to many philosophical systems. Some discussions that offer such arguments, however, are not completely clear whether they take the arguments to show that philosophy should indeed be rejected or modified, sometimes seeming to suggest both that philosophy should be rejected or modified as androcentric, and that it should not.[7] To the extent that they suggest the latter, I have, of course,

6. For some more examples, see Hekman, "Feminization of Epistemology," 70; Wilshire, "Uses of Myth," 93–97; and Gatens, "Feminist Critique of Philosophy," 92–95, and "Modern Rationalism," 22.

7. I find Lloyd's discussion especially difficult to understand, since it includes some statements that seem to contradict each other. On the one hand, as quoted above, Lloyd writes that "our ideals of Reason are in fact male; and if there is a Reason genuinely common to all, it is something to be achieved in the future, not celebrated in the present" (*Man of Reason,* 107), and that "it is clear that what we have in the history of philosophical thought is no mere succession of surface misogynist attitudes, which can now be shed" (103). Similarly, "We have seen that Philosophy has powerfully contributed to the exclu-

no disagreement; I believe, however, that the former view should not be accepted.

2

I believe that the type of argument discussed here should not be accepted for two reasons. The first is that it attributes androcentricity to philoso-

---

sion of the feminine from cultural ideals" (108). This suggests that Lloyd believes philosophy and reason to be androcentric, and therefore, presumably, to require either reform or rejection. However, Lloyd also writes that "feminist unease about ideals of Reason is sometimes expressed as a repudiation of *allegedly* male principles of rational thought" (109; my emphasis). Likewise, "The claim that Reason is male need not at all involve . . . any suggestion that principles of logical thought valid for men do not hold also for female reasoners" (109). And also that "philosophers can take seriously feminist dissatisfaction with the maleness of Reason without repudiating either Reason or Philosophy . . . Philosophy has defined ideals of Reason through exclusions of the feminine. But it also contains within it the resources of critical reflections on those ideals and on its own aspirations" (109). It is unclear why, then, if philosophy has powerfully contributed to the exclusion of the feminine, feminists should not repudiate it.

Perhaps Lloyd means that feminists should not reject all aspects of reason; they should maintain those which enable critical reflections on, and perhaps the reform of, the ideals of reason, and reject the rest. However, this would conflict with her unqualified assertion, cited above, that the principles of logical thought are valid for both men and women (109). Perhaps, then, Lloyd could be understood as proposing that a new, alternative type of reason is to be achieved in the future (108), one that feminists need not reject, and which can be used by men and women alike (109). This suggestion too, however, conflicts with her claim that philosophers and feminists need not repudiate reason, and may continue to use it (109). Lloyd could also be understood as suggesting that feminist criticisms (such as hers) of the associations of reason with masculinity will dissolve the masculine *connotations* of reason, thus enabling us to use reason as it is, but without its masculine connotations. Then we would have a "Reason genuinely common to all" (107), instead of one "deeply affected by, as well as deeply affecting, the social organisation of sexual difference" (108). This last suggestion would explain why Lloyd mentions "the *allegedly* male principles of rational thought" (109; my emphasis): it is not reason itself that is male, only its ideals or connotations. This understanding coheres also with Lloyd's reservations about feminist suggestions for alternative modes of reasoning, supposed to agree more with "femininity" (by emphasizing intuition, emotion, care, and so on), which she takes to preserve the traditional connotations of femininity and masculinity (104–7). She would thus prefer to combat the "feminine" or "masculine" connotations or ideals of reason, rather than reason itself. However, this interpretation conflicts with phrases such as "the maleness of Reason," or "Reason is male" (109), since one would expect Lloyd (according to this interpretation) to see not reason, but only its connotations or ideals as male. This interpretation conflicts also with Lloyd's explicit assertion that "philosophy has been deeply affected by . . . the social organization of sexual difference" (108). This too suggests that not only the masculine ideals or connotations of philosophy have been affected, and hence should be rectified, but also philosophy itself. (Moreover, in her later work Lloyd mentions "the undoubtedly 'male' past of philosophy." See Lloyd, "Feminism in History of Philosophies by using a criterion that is too liberal: it implicates philosophies although they in themselves are not androcentric just because some *other* claims, stereotypes, or social practices, in *other* philosophical (or non-philosophical) contexts are androcentric. The link is too loose. If it is accepted, then by the same logic many other conclusions, some of which would be problematic for the authors of the argument in question, should be accepted as well. Put differently, because the argument is so loose, it can prove too much: it condemns as androcentric not only the preference for reason over emotion, or theory over practice, but also many other notions. Men have been stereotypically associated or identified not only with reason and objectivity but also with initiative, leadership, ability, achievement, courage, creativity, and persistence. If we follow the argumentation above, these qualities too have to be rejected or modified as androcentric. Similarly, the discriminatory, exclusionary social reality has made it more difficult for women not only to engage in activities relating to reason, but also to vote, open bank accounts, criticize their husbands, achieve economic independence, and run for political office. But surely we would not want to take this as reason to designate these activities themselves as androcentric. The same would be true of other exclusionary practices and views, related to other groups. For example, in Europe, at various times and places, Jews were forbidden to own land and so did not engage in agriculture. But we would not take this to show that cultivating land is anti-Semitic. Those who have the social and institutional power sometimes build common stereotypes, conventions, and social practices so that much of what they take to be worthy is associated with or is more accessible to them, and what they take to be less worthy

---

phy," 261.) Lloyd's position, then, remains unclear to me; her discussion seems to suggest both that reason should not be rejected or modified on account of some androcentric identifications or connotations, and that it should.

The same ambivalence is true of Thompson. Some of her claims are quite decisively worded. Thus, she writes that "the Cartesian theory of rationality, by sanctifying science, philosophy and mathematics, removed them further from the reach of women. And even after all these centuries, the odour of sanctity still clings" ("Women and the High Priests of Reason," 13). Moreover, "Cartesianism does not, as far as women are concerned, have much of a potential to liberate" (12). On the other hand, at the end of her paper she presents things less decisively, as questions: "Has the monopoly over the 'high' disciplines, held for so long by an elite group of men, affected their direction or content? What distortions, oversights, omissions have resulted from the limitation on points of view? It is difficult to answer these questions, but impossible to push them aside. After all, if knowledge is going to be merely human knowledge, then why should we settle for less?" (14). Tuana's, Hekman's, Willshire's, and Gaten's discussions, however, are clear on taking these identifications as grounds for seeing philosophy as androcentric.

is associated with or is more accessible to those of less power. But this, of course, is not a good reason for those with less power to accept these associations and social practices, or to reject what may be of worth, thus continuing and even enhancing the discriminatory condition.

Note also that this type of argumentation can be used to prove that many philosophies are gynocentric; claiming that *disfavoring* certain concepts associated with women in one philosophical system has harmed women, implies that *favoring* these concepts in another system has benefited them. For example, if it is accepted that Descartes's reliance on intellect indeed encouraged discrimination against women—identified with emotion and imagination—then we should also accept, by the same argumentation, that Nietzsche's or Kierkegaard's emphasis on emotion and imagination has enhanced women's advancement. If Descartes's position concerning the senses makes his philosophy androcentric or pervasively androcentric, then Locke's position should be seen, by the same token, as making his philosophy gynocentric or pervasively gynocentric. And if abstractions have harmed women, then specific discussions of particular issues, concrete examples, and elaborate distinctions prevalent in, for example, analytic philosophy, have helped women.

Moreover, this type of argumentation can be used to demonstrate that even Cartesianism is gynocentric. Descartes's epistemology stresses reliance on the internal, rather than the external. But women have been associated with the internal. Thus, it could be claimed, Cartesianism and other philosophies enhanced the acceptance of women into circles of learning and improved women's social status. Similarly, Descartes calls for self-restraint, holding that in order not to err we should limit our will to the confines of what we can know. But women have frequently been associated with, and frequently had a public and self-image related to, sexual modesty, temperance, and abstinence. The same is true of other characteristics of Descartes's philosophy: it calls for employing reason with patience and caution, and it is atomistic. But patience and caution are traditionally identified as feminine qualities, and women's lives have often been associated with particular issues and details, while men's with abstractions and general causes.[8] Again, this type of argument emerges as problematic since it proves too much. Its looseness allows us to conclude, too easily and without sufficient basis, that philosophy is andro-

---

8. Such arguments could also be applied to reason at large. For example, some philosophers present the employment of reason as an alternative to, or as the opposite of, reliance on brute force, a practice traditionally associated with men.

centric; but then, this looseness allows us also to reach many other, problematic conclusions.

The second, different (even if related) reason why I suggest that this type of argument should not be accepted is that when sexist and exclusionary social practices put women at a disadvantage concerning a certain philosophical notion, this type of argument rejects as androcentric the philosophical notion, instead of the exclusionary social practices. And when a notion that in itself is not androcentric, and which is not employed androcentrically in a certain philosophy, is employed androcentrically in other contexts (some of them not even philosophical), this type of argument rejects as androcentric the notion or the philosophy, instead of the androcentric employments or contexts.

Thus, surprisingly and notwithstanding what are clearly commendable motivations, the arguments above end up relying on (androcentric) public opinion, social conventions, or social practices as evidence for what is worthy or unworthy, right or wrong. As a general rule it is not a good idea to accept stereotypes, conventions, and common social practices as grounds for deciding whether to accept, reject, or modify philosophical categories. This is all the more so when these are *androcentric* stereotypes, conventions, and social practices. As Martha Nussbaum has pointed out, such arguments, clearly without intending to, yield to and even reinforce androcentric identifications instead of fighting against them.[9]

From the point of view of the history of ideas this is an odd development, since feminism, as a revolutionary movement, has frequently *rejected* arguments from prejudice, social norms, or public and self-images. It has often pursued what it thought was good for women, ignoring what was commonly believed to be so. This is also true for cases where public images and self-images are significant enough to affect people's identities.[10] Feminist theory has frequently refrained from relying on women's

9. "Feminists and Philosophy," 59.

10. For the argument that in order to participate in Descartes's rationality some aspects of women's identities need to be criticized and changed, see Tuana, *Woman and the History of Philosophy*, 41. Tuana's argument seems to me, however, to draw an overly discouraging picture of the demands philosophy would make on women. Thus, concerning Cartesian philosophy, she writes, "A woman who wishes to attain the rational life must put aside *all* that identifies her as female. She must become male" (my emphasis). This claim seems to me exaggerated. It also presupposes that having a rational life is not part of women's being today, or that those who want to employ reason, or practice philosophy, must dedicate all their time to these activities alone. But as Lloyd points out (*Man of Reason*, 47), Descartes believes that one need devote only a few hours a year to "pure thought," and moreover that scientific inquiry (which requires the use of imagination, among other elements) occupies a

identities or self-images in arguments about what to accept, reject, or modify, since many, or even most, women have had strong nonfeminist, and frequently antifeminist, traditional feminine identities. Feminist objectives such as equality, leadership, and empowerment have not been deduced from characteristics believed to be typical of many women's identities or self-images but, on the contrary, have been presented as attributes many women did not yet have but could achieve. One of the main objectives of feminism has been to change the way many women see themselves, and thus to empower and liberate them. And although there is still much work to be done, feminism has indeed succeeded in reducing the preponderance and strength of androcentric stereotypes, self-images, associations, and actual discriminations such as those just mentioned. (Hence, if these arguments for the androcentricity of philosophy *were* to be accepted, there would be fewer reasons today for rejecting or altering philosophy or reason than there used to be. And if the struggle against androcentric prejudices, associations, and practices continues successfully, we can hope that in the future there will be even less of an argument to reject or alter reason and philosophy.)

For these two reasons, I think that this type of argument for the androcentricity (or pervasive androcentricity) of philosophy should not be accepted. It may be answered, however, that according to the definition of androcentricity suggested in the introduction, I have to accept that this argument does show philosophy to be androcentric. This is because the introduction suggests that a philosophy is androcentric if it should be reformed or rejected because it suits men's experiences or minds more than women's, or involves male discrimination against women, or leads to the domination of women by men. And a philosophy that states a preference for a category that is associated androcentrically in other contexts with men rather than women can be seen, at least in some likelihood, to be leading to the domination of women by men. Likewise, a philosophy that states a preference for a category or an activity from which androcentric social reality excludes women can be seen as contributing to the domination of women by men, or to discrimination against women, since now more people will value, or wish to participate in, what women cannot do (or can do with less success). Thus, it may be argued, in spite of the difficulties in the type of argument examined in this chapter, the definition of androcentricity commits me to accepting that this type of argument does correctly identify philosophy as androcentric.

---

middle position between sense and pure thought. (See also Thompson, "Women and the High Priests of Reason," 13–14.)

I believe, however, that this objection should not be accepted. Note that according to the criterion of androcentricity presented in the introduction, a philosophy is androcentric if it *should be reformed or rejected* because it suits men's experiences or minds more than women's, or involves male discrimination against women, or leads to the domination of women by men. This allows us to accept that a philosophy is somehow involved in or leads to the domination of or discrimination against women, yet still judge that its link to the androcentric result is too loose, and its contribution too small, to justify rejection or reform. Not every link in a chain that leads to an unfortunate conclusion should be reformed or rejected. For example, assume that one drives to a concert under the influence of alcohol and causes an accident. It is true that the concert, or even love of music in general, are also somehow involved in the accident, but we do not think that *they* should be reformed or rejected. If the relation is too indirect and weak, and if following the logic of the argument would lead us to condemn almost everything as increasing danger on the road (as well as to laud almost everything as contributing to road safety), we will not suggest that the concert, or music appreciation, should be rejected or reformed as contributing to car accidents. The same, I suggest, it true for the matter at hand.

It may also be argued that there may be arguments of this type where the link between the philosophy and the androcentric result may not be as loose as in the cases above, and hence that rejecting or reforming philosophies as androcentric would not involve all the difficulties presented here. I agree; such cases may be found. Up to now, however, I have not found any; all the examples of the uses of the arguments above I am aware of are too loose.

It may also be suggested that the arguments have been read wrongly. They do not in fact mean to present philosophy, or certain philosophies, as androcentric, but only to point out to us, or draw our attention to the fact, that, in some cases, presenting an innocuous preference for a certain category or activity, although in itself not androcentric, may be related, because of androcentric social practices, images, views, or associations, with androcentricity. I am not sure that it will always be easy to read the arguments discussed in this chapter in such a way, but of course have no objection to doing so. If they are read in this way I have no disagreement with them. My critique, as it was presented earlier, applies only to the reading that takes these arguments to suggest that the philosophies in question are androcentric (as, I believe, these arguments are often read).

3

Arguments from associations and stereotypes appear also in the work of Jacques Derrida and many postmodernist philosophers inspired by him, such as Hélène Cixous or Michèle Le Doeuff.[11] However, in Derrida's influential and celebrated work these arguments are supported by a wider postmodernist theory that, as such, requires a presentation and discussion of its own.

According to Derrida, Western philosophy is pervaded by many binary oppositions.[12] There are many dichotomies, but the most important ones are essential and accidental, central and marginal, typical and atypical, being and nonbeing, presence and absence, pure and impure, stable and changing, certain and doubtful, general and limited, clear and vague, simple and complicated, atomistic and compound, immediate and mediate, original and secondary, conscious and unconscious, real and apparent, serious and playful, internal and external, signified and signifier, literal and metaphorical, spoken and written, voiced and silent, soul and body, meaning and form, intuition and expression, and culture and nature.

Derrida understands these dichotomies to have several characteristics. First, the two terms in each dichotomy have traditionally been taken to be distinct from each other: the essential has traditionally been taken to be distinct from the accidental, the central from the marginal, the signified from the signifier, and so forth.

Second, one of the terms in each dichotomy has traditionally been preferred to the other.[13] The central has traditionally been preferred to the marginal, the pure to the impure, the immediate to the mediate, and so on. Derrida notes some exceptions to such preferences, but claims that they are only exceptions. Moreover, he attempts to show that in certain texts where a preference does not appear to exist, it in fact does.

Third, Derrida claims that the traditionally disfavored term has frequently been conceived as the imperfect, "castrated" version of the favored one. The disfavored term is assumed to have the characteristics of

11. See Cixous, "Sorties," 63–64, and Le Doeuff, "Women and Philosophy," 193–96.

12. This following short description of Derrida's thought does not of course aim to represent all its aspects, but only those most relevant to the arguments for the androcentricity of philosophy.

13. See, for example, *Positions*, 56–57.

the favored one in a partial, imperfect way. Hence, the disfavored term is taken to be conceptually dependent on the favored one.

Fourth, it is not accidental that some terms are preferred to others. The favored terms can be grouped together. For example, presence is traditionally associated with being rather than nonbeing; with consciousness rather than with unconsciousness (what is conscious seems more present to us); with the typical, central, and essential rather than with the atypical, marginal, and accidental (what is typical, central, and essential is more fully and frequently present to us than what is not); with voice, the real, and stable, rather than with silence, the unreal, and the changing (for obvious reasons); with the certain, immediate, and literal rather than the doubtful, mediate, and metaphorical (again for obvious reasons); and with the spoken rather than the written (for reasons to be discussed).[14]

In Derrida's opinion, the existence of these dichotomies in various contexts is frequently tacit, and the preference for the first term over the second is sometimes even denied—as are the connections among the favored terms. To Derrida, the uncovering of these dichotomies and the relations within and among them is part of his philosophical achievement. He labels the tendency in Western philosophy (and Western civilization generally) to prefer the first terms in the dichotomies as "logocentrism."[15] Derrida's overall project is to undermine logocentrism by means of a group of strategies he calls "deconstruction."

Derrida emphasizes certain dichotomies more than others.[16] It has already been shown how the dichotomy of presence and absence is connected to other dichotomies. The phenomenon of "presencing" (of preferring presence to absence) is taken by Derrida to be so important that he calls philosophy "the metaphysics of presencing."[17] Another emphasized dichotomy is that of speaking and writing (*De la grammatologie*, 42–45). Speaking has traditionally been favored over writing,

14. See, for example, *De la grammatologie*, 21–25, and "La Structure," 411.

15. To the best of my knowledge, Derrida never specifies whether in his opinion logocentrism is only or mostly a Western phenomenon. However, he occasionally remarks that a certain logocentric phenomenon pervades *Western* civilization (for example, *Positions*, 19), and he deconstructs only Western texts. At least *prima facie*, however, there is also a strong logocentric element in some Eastern systems of thought (for example, in Confucianism, Hinduism, and Jainism).

16. The status of the emphasized dichotomies in Derrida is not entirely clear. It is uncertain whether they are taken to be more logocentric than others, or to pervade others and actually influence them, or whether the emphasis on these dichotomies is merely a heuristic device for Derrida.

17. See, for example, *De la grammatologie*, 191.

according to Derrida, because the latter has been regarded as an imitation, or signifier, of the former. Moreover, speaking can take place at the time of thinking and thus has an element of immediacy and presencing in it, unlike writing. The preference for speaking over writing, then, matches the preference for signified over signifier, original over imitation, the immediate over the mediate, and presence over absence, and thus is part of the logocentric tradition (23). In Derrida's opinion, however, it is such an important part of logocentrism that it deserves a special name: phonocentrism (ibid.).

A third emphasized dichotomy is masculine/feminine. In this dichotomy, too, the first term is preferred to the second, and is related to first terms in other hierarchies, whereas the second is presumed to be associated with their second terms. Hence, Derrida calls traditional philosophy not only "logocentric" (from *logos*) but also "phallogocentric" (combining *phallus* with "logocentric"). Thus, androcentricity, or as Derrida calls it, phallogocentrism, is shown to be pervasively inherent in Western philosophy.[18]

One of the strategies of deconstruction Derrida employs to cope with the metaphysics of presencing, logocentrism, phonocentrism, phallogocentrism, and so forth is to show that the favored term is in fact never self-sufficient and pure.[19] Derrida argues that the preferred term is always related to the disfavored one and hence is in some sense dependent on it. Thus, one of the arguments that Derrida uses to deconstruct the speaking-writing dichotomy is that writing can do a job that speech cannot: it can technically repeat speech where and when speech itself is not present. But this repeatability is a necessary condition of speaking if speaking is to make sense at all.[20] Derrida seems to argue, perhaps under the influence of Wittgenstein's private language argument, that speech can make sense to us only because it has a fixed meaning, which can be repeated in different contexts. Yet if this essential characteristic of writing—namely repeatability—is a necessary condition of speaking, then writing is not secondary to speaking as Derrida thinks it has traditionally been viewed. On the contrary, speaking is secondary to writing.

18. See, for example, Jacques Derrida, "Avoir l'oreille de la philosophie," interviewed by Lucette Finas, *La Quinzaine littéraire,* November 16, 1972, 16, and "This Strange Institution Called Literature," 57–60.

19. Derrida himself prefers to see the methods of deconstruction not as strategies he employs, but as processes that happen in the text by themselves, and which he merely uncovers.

20. *De la grammatologie,* 65.

Likewise, in what may be called the main body/supplement dichotomy,[21] it is the main body that is traditionally favored. The supplement is taken to be an external, inessential addition to the main body. Hence, whereas the main body is understood to be independent of the supplement and self-sufficient, the supplement is not understood to be independent of the main body. Derrida, however, tries to reverse the traditional relationship between the two concepts. According to his analysis, the supplement can operate as such only because (1) some characteristics are common to it and to the main body and (2) because there is something missing in the main body that can be supplemented. For example, in Rousseau's *Confessions,* writing is needed to supplement speaking, since there is something that both it and speaking can do (namely, emphasize Rousseau's worth as a thinker and a human being), but writing does it better than speaking.[22] Hence, in one sense at least, the supplement is an essential part of the main body and can even be seen as logically prior to it. The deconstruction of this dichotomy is important in Derrida's writings, since once the supplement is emphasized and taken to be prior to the main body, many deconstructions that hitherto seemed absurd appear more plausible.

A close but somewhat different strategy is to show that the distinction between the two terms in a dichotomy does not hold. Once the distinction is collapsed, the two terms are reduced into one. Thus, for example, Derrida claims that since signifieds and signifiers are never completely independent of each other, the distinction between them should not be accepted.[23] Hence, the signifiers should not be understood as referring to signifieds, as they traditionally have been, but only as referring to other signifiers. This deconstruction, too, is important in Derrida's writings. Once signifiers are seen as referring not to signifieds (for example, to physical objects, or intentional states), but only to other signifiers, many of Derrida's deconstructions again seem less absurd. Put differently, once a text is understood as not referring to anything outside itself, it is easier to interpret it in any way one likes.

A third strategy for demonstrating that the favored term is never self-sufficient and pure is to show that it is part of an infinite series of terms, each of which is favored in comparison to some terms and disfavored in comparison to others. There are thus no absolute pure terms (which

21. Derrida himself does not use the term "main body," but only the term "supplement."

22. *De la grammatologie,* 205.

23. *Positions,* 28–30.

might have existed at the ends of the chains if the chains were finite). For example, Derrida shows that for Rousseau writing is a supplement to speech, but speech is a supplement to nonverbal activity. In Rousseau's *Confessions,* the recollections of Maman are a substitute for Maman herself, but Maman in turn is a substitute for the mother, who will also be a substitute for something.[24] On this basis, Derrida concludes that there is an endless chain of such terms, all relative to each other.

A fourth strategy is to apply a distinction reflexively to itself and thus show that it is itself imbued with the disfavored term. For example, Derrida shows that when Aristotle and other philosophers discuss the nature of metaphors (and thereby the distinction between metaphors and nonmetaphors), they use metaphors in the discussions themselves. Hence, Derrida claims, the effort to delineate purely nonmetaphorical communication fails. Nonmetaphorical speech or writing is dependent, in some way, on the metaphorical.[25] Similarly, Derrida points out that philosophers who disfavored writing still use it in the process of explaining and justifying this view.[26]

The deconstruction of the hierarchies of the signified and signifier, main body and supplement, and also of seriousness and playfulness leads Derrida to present further, more iconoclastic strategies of deconstruction. One such is wordplay. Thus, for example, in *La vérité en peinture,* he connects the German word for "I" (*ich*) with the Hebrew word for "man" (in English transliteration: *ish*), since they sound the same, and its phonic converse *chi* to the English *she*.[27] Similarly, in *Glas,* he links Hegel (pronouncing this philosopher's name as in French) with the French word for "eagle" (*aigle*), since they sound almost the same.[28] He likewise links the initials of the French words *"savoir absolu"* (*sa*) with the beginning of the name of the Roman god *Sa*turn, with the French word for "it" (*ça*), and with the French feminine possessive pronoun (*sa*).[29] Note that Derrida does not claim, as Heidegger might have done,

24. *De la grammatologie,* 219–26.
25. "La Mythologie blanche," 301.
26. "La pharmacie de Platon," 182–83.
27. *La vérité en peinture,* 189.
28. *Glas,* 7.
29. *Glas,* 7, 227, 245, 258–59. Derrida later writes: "My friends know that I have composed an entire book with *ça* (the sign of the Saussurian signifier, or Hegel's Absolute Knowing, in French: *savoir absolu,* of Freud's *Id* [the *ça*], the feminine possessive pronoun [*Sa*]). I did not, however, think at the time of the s.a. of speech acts, nor of the problems (formalizable?) of their relation to the signifier, absolute knowing, the Unconscious or even: to the feminine possessive pronoun." Derrida, "Limited Inc, a b c . . ." 254 n. 11.

that one of these words evolved from the other or that they have the same root. He merely relies on the fact that words or parts of words sound almost the same.[30]

Another strategy Derrida uses is based not only on wordplay but also on associations in general. Thus, for example, in *Glas* he associates a throne with a volcano, a toilet seat, and a truncated pyramid.[31] Likewise, in the essay "La Différance" he associates the silence of the *a* in the word *différance* (according to him, this is an unexpressed *a*) with Hegel's *Encyclopaedia,* a pyramid (whose general contour somewhat resembles the shape of the letter *A*), the silence of tombs (the *a* is silent, and the pyramid is a tomb), the "economy of death," and more.[32]

Another deconstructive strategy, which partly overlaps the previous ones, is to use humor, irony, or simply nonsense. In *Spurs* Derrida says that "the text will remain indefinitely open, cryptic, and parodying."[33] Indeed, some of the wordplays and associations he uses provoke the feeling that he is playfully parodying or even ridiculing his readers.

Derrida even uses a new way of writing. Some of his books no longer read in the accustomed way. They do not argue in a more or less organized way for a thesis, and it is frequently difficult and sometimes impossible to decide which parts represent Derrida's own view, and which the views of the authors he writes about; which constitute the predeconstructed text and which the deconstructed one. In some cases, even the physical layout of the writings changes. "Tympan" in *Marges de la philosophie* and the whole of *Glas*, for example, are laid out idiosyncratically. Each page of *Glas* consists of one column that discusses Hegel and another that discusses Genet, and in some cases insertions are added to the columns. Moreover, it is uncertain whether or not the two columns in this deconstructive setting are related.[34]

Derrida takes deconstruction to show that it is wrong to see the disfavored term as a deprived version of the favored one and as dependent upon it. On the contrary, the relationship between the two should be reversed, and the hitherto favored term should be seen as dependent on the hitherto disfavored.[35] But the deconstructive inversion is not to be

30. Of course, although the terms *sound* the same, more or less, they are written differently. It is interesting that Derrida is ready here to favor sound over writing, since such a move might be condemned as phonocentric.
31. *Glas,* 46–47.
32. "La Différance," 3–4.
33. *Spurs,* 137.
34. See also "La Dissémination," 355–57.
35. *Positions,* 56–58.

understood as merely reversing the order of the hierarchy in the dichotomy by switching the places of the favored and the disfavored. Since the
characteristics of the deconstructed, newly understood disfavored term
are now seen as common to both terms, the distinction between them
does not hold and the whole dichotomy collapses. Thus, Derrida says
about this deconstructed, newly understood writing that

> the thesis . . . must forbid a radical distinction between the lin-
> guistic and the graphic sign. . . .
> . . . Now from the moment that one considers the totality of
> the determined signs, spoken, and a fortiori written, as unmoti-
> vated institutions, one must exclude any relationship of natural
> subordination, any natural hierarchy among signifiers or orders
> of signifiers. If "writing" signifies inscription and especially the
> durable institution of a sign (and that is the only irreducible ker-
> nel of the concept of writing), writing in general covers the entire
> field of linguistic signs. In that field a certain sort of instituted
> signifiers may then appear, "graphic" in the narrow and deriva-
> tive sense of the word, ordered by a certain relationship with
> another instituted—hence "written," even if they are
> "phonic"—signifiers.[36]

Predeconstructed speaking and writing, then, can be seen as narrow and
somewhat distorted derivations of deconstructed speaking and writing,
which Derrida, for this reason, sometimes calls "arche-writing."[37]

The same is true for absence in the dichotomy of presence/absence
or supplement in main body/supplement. The hierarchical, dichotomous
distinction between the predeconstructed favored and disfavored terms
collapses when the deconstructed, disfavored term is revealed as basic to
both. Deconstruction functions, then, by bringing to the surface some
tacit aspects of the two terms and thereby introducing a new understanding of their nature. Some of the characteristics of the disfavored terms,
previously taken to constitute their inferiority in dichotomous hierarchies, are seen to be common and essential to both the disfavored and
the favored terms.

The deconstruction does not, however, fully dissolve the hierarchical,
predeconstructed dichotomy. The hierarchical dichotomy is partly re-

---

36. Derrida, *Of Grammatology*, 44. See also *De la grammatologie*, 55.
37. See "La Différance," 14.

tained in the deconstruction, thus constituting an interplay between the predeconstructed and deconstructed dichotomies.[38] This interplay is no harmonious synthesis but a restless movement between dissatisfying emphasis on some aspects and then on others.[39] Derrida calls this interplay "*différance*," a word he created by adding the French noun suffix *-ance* to the verb *différer,* which means both to differ and to defer. According to this understanding, deconstruction does not simply replace a predeconstructed dichotomy with a deconstructed one. The two facets of the dichotomy continue to relate to each other in disharmony.[40] Previous notions and relationships, then, are not completely eliminated in the process of deconstruction. However, their character and significance are critically changed in the new context into which they are put.

Derrida's arguments, like Tuana's or Lloyd's, allow one to considerably broaden the scope of androcentricity. His account suggests that even systems that say nothing of women, or openly oppose androcentricity, are—through such associations and identifications—guilty of androcentricity, simply by virtue of their preference for, for example, the certain over the doubtful, or the real over the apparent. But some of Derrida's methods of deconstruction permit one to extend the scope of androcentricity in philosophy even further than Lloyd's or Tuana's arguments do. The ambiguity of *différance,* as well as the emphasis on signifiers, supplements, and playfulness, rather than on signifieds, main bodies, and seriousness, allow one to "show" that philosophy is androcentric by simply employing wordplay, jokes, or far-fetched analogies according to one's will or whim. Moreover, Derrida's version of the argument by associations, identifications, and stereotypes may seem stronger than Tuana's or Lloyd's, since his version is backed up by a larger general theory, which, if accepted, does not allow the critiques suggested against Tuana's or Lloyd's to arise. One critique was that the arguments are too loose and thus allow a plethora of (sometimes conflicting) conclusions. However, in Derrida's theory this cannot be considered a problem; the plethora of possible conclusions is applauded as one of the main characteristics of the theory. Another critique of Lloyd's and Tuana's arguments was that when androcentric associations are suggested to nonandrocentric views, the androcentric associations, rather than the nonandrocentric views, should be rejected as androcentric. However, this critique presupposes

38. Ibid., 12–14.
39. *Positions,* 56–58.
40. "La Différance," 12–14.

the central/marginal, essential/accidental, or main body/supplement dichotomies. If these dichotomies are rejected, as they are in Derrida's philosophy, this critique cannot arise either.

4

Derrida's theory, like his argument for the androcentricity of philosophy, has been very influential. However, there are many difficulties in it, and these, I believe, render them ineffectual.

Some difficulties are specific: for example, although Aristotle, as well as some other philosophers who discuss the distinction between metaphors and nonmetaphors, uses metaphors in their discussions of this issue, this in itself does not prove that the effort to delineate a purely nonmetaphorical communication must fail. Perhaps the effort does eventually fail; but the fact that Aristotle and a few other authors employed some explicit metaphors in these discussions is not sufficient proof of this. Similarly, the discussion of chains of supplements or substitutes some two or three links long is insufficient to show that these chains go on and on. And although repeatability seems to be essential to both speaking and writing to a more or less similar degree, Derrida's argument does not corroborate his conclusion that one of them is logically prior to the other.

Other difficulties are of a more general nature. Derrida does not represent accurately the views of the authors he discusses and relies on. In his *Strategies of Deconstruction* J. Claude Evans shows how, when drawing on and criticizing Husserl's, Aristotle's, and Saussure's arguments, Derrida ignores relevant parts of their theories and misrepresents and misquotes their views. Geert Lernout shows the same concerning Derrida's treatment of Joyce, and Brian Vickers concerning his treatment of Peirce.[41] Moreover, Derrida concludes too much from the errors in beliefs he incorrectly presents as widely accepted. Many dichotomies, in many contexts, do not require, in order to make sense, the presupposition that the notions employed in them are conceptually independent of each other. Thus Derrida's argument that notions are not independent of each other does not collapse the dichotomies. And even if, for some reason, the dichotomies did collapse once it was shown that the terms employed in them are not independent of each other, the dichotomies could just

41. Lernout, *The French Joyce,* 57–66; Vickers, "Derrida's Reading of C. S. Peirce."

disintegrate; they would not have to transmute to the state of *différance* or aporetic interplay between the deconstructed and predeconstructed dichotomies that Derrida envisages.

Moreover, many of Derrida's general descriptions of Western culture or philosophy seem incorrect and overgeneralized. Derrida, who criticizes the Western philosophical urge to find sameness in everything, nevertheless treats all Western philosophy as if it were uniform. However, as Jean Grimshaw argues (in a slightly different context), philosophy is highly varied.[42] True, some concepts traditionally and frequently have been preferred to others. This is the case, for example, with being and nonbeing, or reality and appearance. It is less true, however, of notions such as simple and complicated, spoken and written, intuition and expression, atomistic and compound, internal and external, immediate and mediate, meaning and form, or culture and nature. On some occasions the first terms in these dichotomies have been preferred to the second, but on others the second have been preferred to the first. We do not always prefer the simple to the complicated, or the atomistic to the compound. In many contexts, the voice is not preferred to script but, on the contrary, written documents are preferred to oral claims, reports, and agreements, and the "written language" is preferred to the "spoken language," which is considered more colloquial. In some cases, the signified is preferred to the signifier, and in others not. Some people prefer art to the original, and many prefer words to what they express. In many cases, culture has been preferred to nature, but in others—such as the Romantics, or Rousseau—it has not. And materialists such as Leucippus, Democritus, Hobbes, and Carnap did not prefer mind to matter.

Nor has one of these notions always been understood or conceived in terms of the other: this is the case, for example, with intuition and expression, atomistic and compound, internal and external, immediate and mediate, meaning and form, culture and nature, and mind and matter. Furthermore, texts can prefer the same terms without preferring the same concepts. "Nature" has different, and to an extent contradicting, meanings for the Romantics, the empiricists, and Aquinas. "Freedom" has different meanings for Aristotle, Eckhart, and Mill. The same is true for other frequently used—and therefore rich and ambivalent—concepts, such as "power," "reality," "knowledge," "being," "goodness," "man," and "woman." As is discussed by Simone de Beauvoir, among others,

---

42. The variability in philosophy is discussed by Grimshaw in her criticism of an argument by Sheila Ruth. See Grimshaw, *Philosophy and Feminist Thinking*, 66–69.

there are many contradictions in the common representations and associations of women and men.[43] Women, like men, have been associated with both nature and culture, goodness and evil, desire and temperance. For this reason, Derrida can place man on the side of nature, and woman on the side of culture, whereas Hélène Cixous, with equal justification, puts woman on the side of nature, and man on that of culture.[44]

Derrida's attempt to group together concepts in order to have some of them imply others is also problematic. The preference for the original over the secondary, for example, coheres well with the preference of the signified over the signifier, or the literal over the metaphorical, but is in conflict with the preference for the cultural over the natural. In some other cases, it is not clear that any relation—either of agreement or of tension and conflict—exists between dichotomies. Such is the case, for example, with the relation of internal/external with typical/atypical. The problem becomes even more acute when it is remembered that the terms Derrida presents as preferred are, in fact, not always preferred, and that they sometimes have different meanings in different contexts. Note also that by using Derrida's argumentation, one can claim that Western philosophy not only seems to worsen women's condition, but also to enhance goodness and justice. Goodness/evil and justice/injustice are again traditional dichotomies in each of which the first term has been preferred to the second.

Because of these difficulties, it seems to me that Derrida's deconstructive theory, and the argument for the androcentricity of philosophy it incorporates, cannot be accepted.[45]

43. See Beauvoir, *Second Sex,* pt. 3, chap. 9.
44. Cixous, "Sorties," 63. On p. 64, however, Cixous may again be putting man on the side of nature.
45. The terms "deconstruction" and "deconstructive" have also begun to be used by nonpostmodernists and outside postmodernist discourse (see, for example, Okin, "Gender," 78–83, and Williams, "Deconstructing Gender," 797, 839, 840). In such cases, the terms are employed to denote analysis and rejection of dogmatic, one-dimensional, and simplistic explanations that ignore the complexity of the phenomena they discuss. Although such nonpostmodernist "deconstructions" are similar to postmodernist ones in rejecting dogmatism and oversimplification, they differ radically in the methods they employ. While postmodernist deconstructions celebrate opaqueness and lack of clarity, the nonpostmodernist "deconstructions" do not strive to be vague, and are frequently—as in the case of Okin and Williams—clear and cautious. While postmodernist deconstructions use *différance,* sometimes far-fetched analogies, and word plays, the nonpostmodernist ones employ methods such as carefully examining the phenomena discussed, showing possible contradictions and ambiguities, or distinguishing between different meanings of what is said. While postmodernist deconstructions are dogmatic—they accept neither clear and simple

5

It may be objected, however—following understandings of Derrida's theory presented by, for example, Richard Rorty and John Scanlon—that the reservations regarding Derrida's philosophy I suggest here, and my very presentation of his philosophy, are misguided.[46] They are too logocentric, and present Derrida as entering upon argument and conclusion, explanation and explicandum, while in fact his discussion is deliberately playful and anarchistic in its very essence. Thus, Derrida's philosophy cannot be grasped or explained, a fortiori, not judged, by the use of rational tools. According to this view, then, one should take more seriously (to use this term tongue-in-cheek) the claim in *Spurs* that "the text will remain indefinitely open, cryptic, and parodying" (137).

This is a possible interpretation of Derrida's texts, and for those who accept Derrida according to this latter understanding, many of the criticisms I have suggested are, indeed, not to the point at all. The postmodernist readiness to rely on jokes, wordplay, and far-fetched analogies, or simply vagueness, irrationality, and lax argumentation, allows a great number and a wide variety of arguments for almost any thesis, including theses concerning the androcentricity of philosophy. However, I believe that on this understanding, too, Derrida's theory, and its argument for the androcentricity of philosophy, should not be accepted.

One way of explaining my reservations with this type of argument is to point out that I will not accept it in many other circumstances. Suppose I am trying to decide whether or not to support a suggested national, economic, or social policy (relating to, for example, welfare, gun prohibition, or legalized abortions). Or that I have to deliberate about a candidate for a political office, or for a fellowship in the university. Or assume

---

claims even when they are justified, nor generalizations even where, and to the extent, they are warranted—nonpostmodernist "deconstructions" try to remain faithful to reality. Moreover, the methods used in nonpostmodernist "deconstructions" precede postmodernist deconstruction; historians, philosophers, sociologists, and so on had noted the importance of caution, subtlety, sensitivity to complexities, and the rejection of simplified generalizations long before Derrida. I believe the term "deconstruction" is redundant in nonpostmodernist contexts. If it is used, however, the differences between it and postmodernist deconstruction should be kept in mind.

46. Scanlon, "Pure Presence"; Rorty, "Is Derrida a Transcendental Philosopher?" Rorty discusses two schools in Derrida interpretation, the one admiring him for "having given us rigorous arguments for surprising philosophical conclusions," the other emphasizing the "the playful, distancing, oblique way in which Derrida handles traditional philosophical figures and topics" (235).

that I have to make up my mind about a personal, economic, or career decision. Suppose also that someone were to suggest to me arguments based on jokes, wordplay, far-fetched analogies, or simply vagueness, irrationality, and lax argumentation, as reasons for buying or refraining from buying a house, or electing this or that candidate for a political office or a fellowship, or supporting a certain social or economic policy. Should I treat this argumentation seriously? The reply, I think, is clear. I take nonserious argumentation to be, well, nonserious. If the argumentation is a joke, I will treat it so. I do not see why the situation is different when coming to consider the androcentricity of philosophy.

This seems to me sufficient for rejecting this argument for the androcentricity of philosophy. It may be answered, however, that this critique is deficient, since it only asserts that in other cases, too, arguments based on jokes or wordplay or vagueness are not acceptable, without explaining what is problematic in them. It should be added, then, that these arguments are problematic because they are not informative, are not to the point, discuss issues that are irrelevant to the question one is deliberating about, and by using them almost anything could be proven about almost everything. Such methods could be used with the same degree of success and reliability to prove also that philosophy—any philosophy—is nonandrocentric, or gynocentric, or that it is geared toward the benefit of the working class, or that of the bourgeoisie, or of people whose family name starts with the letter Z. Put differently, those who accept such modes of argumentation will be able to accept any argument or claim for the androcentricity of philosophy according to whim. But in so doing, they also open the door to an acceptance, by themselves or by others, of almost any proposition or claim whatsoever. Arguments from whim, vagueness, or irrationality are all irrefutable—but because of this are also useless. One might as well avoid the trouble of presenting arguments in support of one's claims, and just say: I accept this claim because I feel like it.[47]

What I have written here about Derrida-inspired methods of "proving everything about anything" is true also of these methods when they are inspired by other writers, such as Heidegger, Lacan, Lyotard, and Deleuze. They, it seems to me, cannot be relied on either. Joanna Hodge, for example, employs a Heidegger-inspired argument to show the androcen-

47. In my discussion of Derrida I have concentrated on problems relating to claims about the androcentricity of philosophy. For a discussion of the general unhelpfulness for feminism of much postmodernist discourse, see Fricker, "Feminism in Epistemology."

tricity of Descartes's philosophy. According to her, Descartes constructs bodies in general as "mechanical structures, appended to some rational processes."[48] But insofar as women's bodies are understood in this way, the "rational process is not taking place in the mind of the woman to whom that mechanical structure is appended, but in the minds of men. The bodies of women are thus constituted as appendages of men's desire, not as the appendages of rational processes attributable to women." Thus women, unlike men, cannot accompany the author of the *Meditations* from doubt to certainty:

> Women therefore have a reason for doubting the existence of an objective world, as women have a reason for doubting that there is available to them a body, in which their rational processes are incorporated, since both world and body are culturally constructed by men as belonging not to women but to men. Women are put by the Cartesian system in the position of the insane person, who cannot see the laughability of Cartesian doubt. Thus in the Cartesian system there is already inscribed the position of the humourless feminist, who cannot see the joke. (162–63)

Likewise, Luce Irigaray discusses Spinoza's first definition in part 1 of his *Ethics*.[49] Spinoza's definition is: "By cause of itself, I understand that, whose essence involves existence; or that, whose nature cannot be conceived unless existing" (83). Irigaray writes that this definition means also

> that which by nature can be conceived only as existing, or: *that which provides its own envelope* by turning its essence outward, must *necessarily* exist. That which provides its own space-time necessarily exists.
>
> Hence:
>
> —We do not exist *necessarily* because we do not provide ourselves with our own envelopes.
>
> —Man would thus exist more necessarily than woman because he gets his envelope from her. (83–84; Irigaray's emphases).

48. "Subject, Body and the Exclusion of Women from Philosophy," 162.
49. Irigaray, "The Envelope."

Similarly, Sabina Lovibond shows how Rosi Braidotti writes on the same page both that "radical feminists philosophers do not argue for the implicitly moral value of the feminist standpoint" and that "the feminist philosophical position of difference has the . . . merit . . . of *denouncing the injustice accomplished against women.*"[50] Likewise, Braidotti analyzes the oppression of women in terms of "concrete exploitation," and writes that feminism aims at "the acquisition of basic socio-political rights," yet at the same time praises Deleuze because he "finally puts a stop to the traditional search for ideas . . . which are 'just' (in theory and politics alike)," and writes, moreover, that "ideas . . . can be neither 'just' or 'false.'"[51] Again, while on the one hand she criticizes what she takes to be rationalist "paranoia" and "aggression," on the other hand she has doubts about "the coherence and therefore the accessibility" of Cixous's thought, disapproves of Le Doeuff's style, since it is "impossible to locate [Le Doeuff] in one specific position," and employs "the language of Enlightenment modernism."[52]

For the reasons I have given, I cannot see such arguments as helpful for deciding whether or not philosphy is androcentric.

50. Braidotti, *Patterns of Dissonance*, 264; discussed in Lovibond, "Feminism and the 'Crisis of Rationality,'" 81; Lovibond's emphasis.
51. Braidotti, *Patterns of Dissonance*, 210, 145, 125; Lovibond, "Feminism," 81.
52. Braidotti, *Patterns of Dissonance*, 242, 198; Lovibond, "Feminism," 81.

4

Harmful Philosophical Notions

I

Another type of argument for the androcentricity of philosophy claims that some philosophical notions are androcentric because they manipulate, objectify, or disempower women not through these notions' association with stereotypes or social practices, as in the previous chapter, but through the harm they inflict on women in more direct ways. This form of argument discusses how some notions are actually employed in androcentric ways, or lead to such employment. As in the previous chapter, here too, the argument discusses philosophical notions that *prima facie* are not androcentric, such as objectivity or abstraction. And it does not merely point out that a certain notion was used in a certain case in an androcentric manner (for example, that the notion of objectivity was used in a certain case to argue that it is objectively true that women are inferior to men). Such cases of explicit androcentric claims have already been discussed in Chapter 2. Like the argument discussed in the previous chapter, the one discussed here aims to make a wider claim. It suggests that because of such applications, within or outside philosophy, the notion itself, in all its uses, is androcentric.[1] If accepted, this argument, too, would render philosophy pervasively androcentric. It would suggest that many notions, some of them widely used in philosophy, are androcentric in all their applications.

Various versions of this argument are used in order to claim that a

---

1. As in the other chapters, here too, such arguments sometime appear in contexts whose main focus is not the androcentricity of philosophy, but other issues in feminist philosophy.

notion itself, rather than a particular use of it, is androcentric. One version bases itself on the actual harmful uses of the notion in question. Elisabeth Young-Bruehl, for example, writes that "recent feminists have said—to speak baldly—why emulate male rationality? Male rationality, after all, has been supplying reasons—for centuries—for the oppression of women; why emulate it? Male rationality has judged women's mental abilities—as well as their physical abilities—inferior; why emulate it?"[2] Likewise, Beverly Thiele condemns abstractions, generalizations, and universalizations, since theorists have employed them to ignore what seemed to them unimportant—frequently, women's issues—and to portray a picture of reality that accords with a male understanding of what is significant.[3] She also censures the notion "nature," since scholars have employed it to convince women that some misogynist views are, in fact, undeniably correct. This was possible since "the 'natural' ceases to require a social or political explanation; it is simply given, a constant which can be taken for granted" (36). To rectify such distortions, Thiele calls for a new gynocentric theory that "not only challenges and transforms the *content* of political philosophy; it also challenges and transforms its *methodology*. In taking off from our critique of male-stream thought we are sensitized to the political uses of the male-stream magic tricks and do not have to perform on the same terms" (41–43; Thiele's emphases).

The argument seems to be based on induction; it generalizes from some harmful uses of a notion to all uses. It seems to work thus:

1. Some uses of notion X are harmful to women.
2. Conclusion: All uses of notion X are harmful to women.

I do not think that this argument can be accepted because, as Janet Radcliffe Richards points out, "the fact that something can be put to a bad use does not show that it is bad in itself."[4] This argument for the androcentricity of philosophy is problematic, not only because of deeper, Humean problems in induction, which hold even when all cases we are aware of follow a certain regularity, but also because the argument generalizes from a few cases to all in spite of many counterexamples. Consider, for example, the argument against abstractions and universalizations. Some abstractions and universalizations have, indeed, been put to andro-

---

2. "Education of Women," 13. Young-Bruehl herself does not seem to accept this view.
3. "Vanishing Acts," 35–36.
4. *Sceptical Feminist*, 49.

centric uses. As Martha Nussbaum and Sabina Lovibond show, however, some abstractions and generalizations have also assisted women's liberation.[5] Such would be, for example, "all people have a right to vote," "all human beings have a right to property," or "the dignity of all people should be respected." There are also many cases where universalizations and generalizations have neither harmed nor assisted women, but were used in ways unrelated to the issue of women's liberation or empowerment. The argument, however, generalizes from the androcentric uses to all uses, while ignoring those that have benefited women or have neither benefited nor harmed them.[6]

It should also be noted that not only universalization but also its alternative, particularization, has been used in ways harmful to women. Certain particularizations, such as claims about women's different interests, social positions, and capacity for knowledge have been used at various times to argue that women's actual interests are domestic only, that they should defer to men, and that they should not be admitted to universities. Although one avenue to discrimination may be through generalizations that falsely present the characteristics or interests of some as pertinent to all, a no less likely avenue is the claim that different groups of people should be treated differently. It would seem, moreover, that more women in the world have suffered from receiving unjustified unequal treatment than from receiving unjustified equal treatment. The degree of the harm suffered because of the former also seems to exceed that caused by the latter. Of course, just as we should not reject all applications of a notion because of some in the case of particularization, so we should not do it in the case of universalization.

What has been written here about abstractions is also true of the notion "nature." Both "nature" and "culture" have been misused to manipulate women into believing that they are inferior to men, and "nature" has also been employed in ways that have helped women (for example, in "natural rights" theory). The same is true of any or almost any other notion. It is difficult to think of any notion that could not be—or has not been—employed to harm women in some ways, and to help them in others (as well as to enhance or obstruct many other ends). It seems more plausible, then, to reject specific incorrect uses of notions and accept specific correct ones, than to reject, because of some wrong applications,

5. Nussbaum, "Human Functioning and Social Justice"; Lovibond, "Feminism and Pragmatism," esp. 70–73.

6. This is a problematic move for the argument to take, since it itself generalizes and abstracts. But I will not pursue this here.

whole notions with all their negative and positive uses. Such rejection precludes our ability to benefit from the positive employments of the notions.

It may be suggested that perhaps this argument for the androcentricity of philosophy should be read, or reconstructed, differently, as saying that although there is nothing problematic with the notions themselves, and they frequently do not lead to androcentric uses, we should notice that they have sometimes been used in androcentric ways, and be sensitive of such possible applications in the future. This more moderate reading of the argument is, of course, stronger (as most moderate suggestions are), and I fully endorse it.

2

In other versions of the argument, the claim that a notion is androcentric is based not on certain bad uses that it was put to, but on something in the character of the notion in question that, it is claimed, leads it to function in an androcentric way. Arguments of this type can be presented in the following way:

1. There is something in the character of notion X that leads it to be used in ways harmful to women.
2. Conclusion: All uses of notion X are harmful to women, and it should be rejected or reformed.

This version of the argument is stronger than the previous one, since it relies not merely on noting some cases where a notion has been used in a way that harmed women, but on a relation claimed to exist between the character of the notion and its harmful applications. Catharine MacKinnon, for example, writes that

> unpacking the feminist approach to consciousness revealed a relation between one means through which sex inequality is produced in the world and the world it produces; the relation between objectification, the hierarchy between self as being and other as thing, and objectivity, the hierarchy between the knowing subject and the known object. Epistemology and politics

emerged as two mutually enforcing sides of the same unequal coin.[7]

As the terms are commonly used, people objectify others when they treat others as nonautonomous objects, who have no thoughts, choices, and motivations of their own, and people are taken to be objective to the extent they succeed in being impartial and minimizing the projection of their subjective prejudices and wishes onto the matter of their thought. For MacKinnon, the link between the notion and the harm, it seems, is that both objectivity and objectification, the "two mutually enforcing sides of the same unequal coin," involve hierarchies, one between the knowing subject and the known object (where the former takes itself to be superior to the latter), the other between the self as being and the other as thing. Hence knowing objectively, or trying to do so, will involve or breed objectification.

MacKinnon suggests another link between the notion and the harm in her *Toward a Feminist Theory of the State*, where she writes that "objectivity, as the epistemological stance of which objectification is the social process, creates the reality it apprehends by defining as knowledge the reality it creates through its way of apprehending it" (114). Here MacKinnon seems to suggest, possibly under some kind of Kantian influence, that whatever people, or men, take to be objectively true is also created by them as reality, and whatever they create as reality is taken to be objectively true; and if it is accepted that men have a tendency to objectify, it is probable that they will create reality (which they will take to be objective) in a way that objectifies women.

Lorraine Code, too, presents the characteristics of a philosophical notion that leads to harmful political phenomena. She discusses not objectivity as such, but the subject-object relation as it is endorsed in what she calls the autonomy-of-reason credo, and not objectification, but control and manipulation:

> The subject-object relation that the autonomy-of-reason credo underwrites is at once its most salient and its most politically significant epistemological consequence. The relation pivots on

7. *Toward a Feminist Theory of the State*, xi. To show that objectivity is androcentric one has to show also that objectification presents a problem especially to women. But since I believe that the argument is already too problematic in its first part, which relates objectivity to objectification, I will not examine this second issue here.

two assumptions: that there is a sharp split between subject and object and that it is a primary purpose of cognitive activity to produce the ability to control, manipulate, and predict the behavior of its objects. . . .

> The established subject-object relation in epistemologies that aspire to the scientific ideal is a distanced, neutral, separated one, and in all of these aspects it is asymmetrical. The subject is removed from, detached from, positions himself at a distance from the object; and knows the object as other than himself. Unidirectional observation is the primary subject-object relation—a relation best maintained vis-à-vis medium-sized objects in the physical world or microscopic objects available for scientific observation, quantification, and measurement. . . . Theorists of the autonomy-of-reason persuasion assume that neither the subject nor the object will be changed or otherwise affected in an act of knowing. *Understanding* the object of inquiry, where it figures at all among epistemic concerns, is of minimal significance. In fact, a subject's demonstrated ability to manipulate, predict, and control the behavior of his objects of knowledge is commonly regarded as the evidence par excellence that he knows them.[8]

Part of the discussion is confusing, since the claim that "a subject's demonstrated ability to manipulate, predict, and control the behavior of his objects of knowledge is commonly regarded as the evidence par excellence that he knows them" seems to be in tension with the claim that "theorists of the autonomy-of-reason persuasion assume that neither the subject nor the object will be changed or otherwise affected in an act of knowing." Perhaps, however, the discussion here concerns two different types or branches of subject-object relation underwritten by the autonomy-of-reason credo, or perhaps there is another explanation for this. Either way, what is characteristic of this mode of knowledge is that it emphasizes the asymmetry as well as difference and detachment between the knower and the known, typical also of cases of control and manipula-

---

8. *What Can She Know?* 139–40; Code's emphasis. Code's book critiques mainly modern Anglo-American philosophy (xi), but "the autonomy-of-reason persuasion," adduced at the beginning of the quotation as underwriting the subject-object relation, is also found in Plato, Descartes, and Kant (112–16). It should be noted, as it was concerning MacKinnon's argument, that various further steps have to be taken in order to show that control and manipulation are androcentric, but as before, I will ignore this issue in the present discussion.

tion, where manipulators detach themselves, and deem themselves very different, from what they manipulate.

Another example is presented by Elizabeth Gross, who takes feminist theory to be "a refusal of a number of central values, concepts and operations necessary for the functioning of patriarchal theory, and an affirmation of the alternatives to these given forms of discourse."[9] Among the former are

> commitments to objectivity, observer-neutrality, and the context-independence as unquestioned theoretical values. . . . Objectivity is considered as a form of interchangeability or substitutionability of observers or experimenters, as a check against individual bias. This ideal of interchangeability is based on the assumption of a similarity of viewpoint and position between observers—who must be "appropriately trained." This assumption is necessarily blind to the different structural positions men and women occupy, their different degrees of access to suitable training, and their (possibly) different relations to their disciplines. The neutrality and universality of many patriarchal discourses presumed in the social sciences is thus sex-blind—unable to acknowledge the different social positions of men and women in presuming a neutral, interchangeable subject. (199)

Here the harm caused by the notions (objectivity, observer-neutrality, and context-independence) is not explicitly stated, but I take it that Gross means that not acknowledging the different social positions held by men and women may conceal from women their specific interests, which are related to these social positions, as well as the very fact that they hold different (and frequently disadvantaged) positions in society. Thus, observer neutrality, and so on, help to conceal from women facts or ideas that could liberate or empower them, or help to convince women of ideas that subjugate them.

This version of the argument is based, then, not on simple extrapolation from some harmful applications to all, but on the way a certain characteristic in the notion in question leads to androcentric applications. However, this version of the argument is also problematic. The characteristic pointed out may allow, in some cases, the use of the notion in an

9. "Conclusion," 198.

androcentric way; but it does not make *all* uses of the notion androcentric, so that we should reject as androcentric the notion itself. To see this we do not need to pry into the claimed link; it is sufficient to see that there are many counterexamples, where the notions or categories relate to nonandrocentric, rather than androcentric, results. And if there are such counterexamples, then one cannot automatically infer from the existence of these categories or notions that androcentric results follow, and one needs to examine specific cases, one by one, and reject or reform as androcentric only those that indeed lead to androcentricity.

Take the example of objectivity and objectification. People who try to be objective sometimes adopt mistaken views that present women as nonautonomous objects or mere means. However, the effort to be objective sometimes liberates people from prejudices leading to the objectification of women, and many people who try to be objective, or endorse the notion of objectivity, do not hold these mistaken views about women. Again, a man who objectifies women, for example, a rapist, may take his views to be objectively right (thinking that women are "objectively" instruments of his pleasure). Yet he may just as well not have such an ethos, and think that what he does simply serves his subjective whim, without caring or thinking at all about what he would see as objectively right or wrong. He may even think that what he does is objectively wrong, and still do it. One can be objective without objectifying, and one can objectify without trying to be objective. These examples, and many others that one can readily think of, suggest that being objective is neither a sufficient nor a necessary condition for objectification. Both bad and good actions can result from both subjectivist and objectivist claims and attitudes. MacKinnon's argument about the link between objectivity and objectification may also seem problematic for other reasons. One usually does not feel any hierarchical superiority toward the objects of one's thought when one tries to think, objectively or nonobjectively, about, for example, utilitarianism or alpha particles. And even if there were some kind of hierarchical relation between the knowing subject and the known object, it need not lead to objectification; not all hierarchies involve objectification.[10] (It also is not clear how, or in what sense, utilitarianism or alpha particles could be objectified.) All this suggests that the characteristics of objectivity *may,* but do not have to, lead to objectification.

The same is true for cases where the knowing subject sees herself or

10. Relationships between parents and children, or teachers and students, for example, almost always involve hierarchy, but may or may not involve objectification.

himself as very different from the known object, as in Code's argument presented earlier. There are many counterexamples: many people think about, say, utilitarianism, alpha particles, scientific realism, Immanuel Kant or Virginia Woolf, and many other objects of thought while being aware that they (the thinkers) are very different from what they are thinking about. In some cases such thoughts are related to control and manipulation, but very frequently they are not. One may think about Woolf, for example, with admiration for her ability and achievement, or sorrow for her suffering and death, or curiosity about the similarities and differences between her style and James Joyce's, with no manipulation and control involved.

The same is true for the awareness that while one knows something, one's object of knowledge does not know one. This asymmetry may be accompanied by a feeling of superiority and may involve control and manipulation, but does not have to. It could involve a feeling of wonder or mere intellectual curiosity without involving manipulation and control. We may, for example, think about, say, Plato's universals while being aware that they, of course, are not thinking about us. If not all cases where the knowing subject sees herself or himself as different from the known object lead to manipulation and control, we have to continue to examine each case individually.

This is also true for the third argument. Many people who accept the interchangeability, observer-neutrality, and context-independence paradigms reach the conclusion that there are some differences in women's and men's social positions, that women face discrimination in some ways, and that there is some dissimilarity between some of women's and men's interests. They believe that women and men fill different positions in, say, American society, and that this claim is true regardless of either one's background and political or religious views or the context of discussion. On the other hand, similarly to what has been argued earlier concerning the subjectivist and objectivist attitudes, one can reject the interchangeability, observer-neutrality, and context-independence paradigm and explain that, from his or her point of view and in the context of his or her culture or biography, women do not face discrimination at all and have nothing to complain about, or that women and men indeed have distinct social positions and that this is the way it should be, since women should be subservient to men. As above, here too, the argument that suggests that, because of a certain characteristic, some notions are androcentric in their nature, or in all their applications, is unsuccessful.

It may be suggested, however, that I have misunderstood these arguments. For example, the argument that discussed the difference between subject and object was meant to imply not that all cases where the subject differs from the object lead to control and manipulation, but that only some of them do, and that, in such cases, the androcentric applications are linked with specific characteristics in these notions. The same is true of the other arguments. If this is the correct reading of these arguments, they are unobjectionable. I should like to point out, however, that not only the notions discussed in these arguments but also their "converse" notions (for example, not only subject-object difference but also subject-object similarity; not only objectivism but also subjectivism), and probably almost any philosophical notion whatsoever, have some androcentric, as well as some feminist, applications.

Sally Haslanger has made just such a suggestion concerning MacKinnon's objectivity-objectification claim. (Haslanger does not present this suggestion as a reading of MacKinnon, but as a more moderate, and hence stronger, reconstruction of MacKinnon's claims.) Haslanger distinguishes between seeing objectivity as strongly masculine, namely, that "satisfying the norms of objectivity is sufficient, at least under conditions of male dominance, for being a sexual objectifier," and seeing objectivity as weakly masculine, namely, that "those who function as men [in an objectifying way] are successful in this role, at least in part, because they are objective."[11] She disagrees with MacKinnon's view that objectivity is strongly masculine (109, 111–13). However, she believes that objectivity is weakly masculine, since in various ways it can contribute to the objectification of women (105–9). For example, it can help objectifiers to present various views and observations as neutral, and ignore their own effect on what they observe (106). Employing a somewhat similar argument, Haslanger takes objectivity to relate also to what she calls "collaboration in objectifying"—that is to say, cases where something is treated as "an object that has by nature properties which are a consequence of objectification" (109), but without being viewed in terms of projected desires, or having people's views forced upon the object (109–11). I agree with this argument, but would like to point out that objectivity—like most or almost all other notions—can contribute also to almost any other social phenomenon. Using such criteria, it is as plausible to label objectivity as "weakly masculine" as it is to label it "weakly feminine," "weakly democratic," "weakly fascist," "weakly helpful," or "weakly obstruc-

---

11. "On Being Objective and Being Objectified," 102.

tive." I believe that the same is true of "collaboration in objectifying." Almost any notion can be characterized by "collaboration in objectifying," as well as "collaboration in liberating" or "collaboration in resisting objectification."

3

It may also be suggested, however, that these arguments should be read in yet another, more moderate and stronger way. For example, Code's arguments may be read as suggesting that subject-object dissimilarity does not *always* lead to control and manipulation, but that it is merely more *prone* to lead to control and manipulation than is subject-object similarity. Likewise, Thiele may perhaps be read as arguing that abstractions are merely more likely to lead to harmful consequences for women than specifications, and MacKinnon as proposing that the effort to achieve objectivity is merely more likely to lead to objectification than the effort to remain nonobjective. Similarly, Gross may be understood as suggesting only that observer neutrality is more prone than observer nonneutrality to lead to blindness to the way women are discriminated against, or to women's and men's different social positions. This type of argument can be presented thus:

1. A certain notion is more prone to androcentric uses than its alternatives.
2. Conclusion: The notion should be seen as more androcentric than its alternatives, and hence, from the androcentricity/non-androcentricity point of view, should not be opted for.

This type of argument, then, does not suggest that all uses of a certain notion are androcentric, but only that it is more prone to be used androcentrically than other notions are. Hence, at least when there are alternatives, and all other things being equal, the notion in question should not be used. (Of course, it is not always the case that there are viable alternatives, and it is frequently not the case that "all other things" are equal. But to simplify the discussion, let us disregard these factors.) Since this type of argument does not suggest that the notion is always employed in androcentric ways, but only that it is more likely, or prone, to be employed so than alternative notions are, the critiques in the two previous sections do not apply to it. It is insufficient here to point out that many of the uses of the notion are not androcentric, and that one cannot infer from some androcentric application to all applications or to the character of the notion itself, since the present type of argument does not claim that all uses are androcentric, only that the notion is more prone to androcentric uses than its alternatives.

However, claims concerning the higher likelihood of notions to lead to androcentric uses are frequently doubtful. How can it be shown that a certain notion is more prone to androcentric uses than another? One way of trying to do so is to examine the ratio between the actual androcentric and the actual neutral and gynocentric uses of that notion, and compare it to the ratio between the actual androcentric and the actual neutral and gynocentric uses of alternative notions. Thus, for example, one would have to examine the ratio between the number of discussions where subject-object *dissimilarity* relates to *control* and the number of discussions where subject-object *dissimilarity* relates to *libratory themes,* and compare it to the ratio between the number of discussions where subject-object *similarity* relates to *control* and the number of discussions where subject-object *similarity* relates to *libratory themes.* This, however, would be very difficult to do. Moreover, it will be insufficient, since in order to substantiate claims concerning proneness one should take into account not only the actual androcentric, neutral, and gynocentric uses of the compared notions, but also their *possible* uses, and estimate the *likelihood* that these uses would be actualized. All this is too complicated and imprecise to yield reliable results.

One could also rely on what might be loosely called the "logic" of the notion in question, by focusing on its characteristics that make it more amenable than other notions to androcentric uses. However, this too is problematic. On the one hand, we have a general philosophical notion (for example, observer neutrality) that in itself is *prima facie* not androcentric. On the other hand, we have an androcentric view or practice (for example, blindness to or denial of women's and men's different average economic positions within American society). The former *can* lead to the latter, but the link is loose. The latter cannot be deduced from the former alone. Some suppositions have to be added in order to move from one to the other. But it is not clear that these further suppositions will be added, or that they are likely to. Moreover, thinkers who see that certain added suppositions can lead them from the philosophical notion (for example, observer neutrality) to an androcentric application (for example, blindness to or denial of women's and men's different economic positions within American society) may reject one or more of these suppositions in order to avoid this undesirable result, while still endorsing the general philosophical notion. Arguments claiming that some general philosophical notions are more prone to androcentric uses than are the alternatives, then, seem to be problematic as well.

Some of the authors who present the arguments discussed in this chapter may be seeing the androcentric applications as merely the superficial symptoms, and the philosophical notions as the deeper illness, which has to be eradicated so that the symptoms will not reappear. But if what I have written in this chapter is correct, the androcentric views are the illness and symptoms together. The notions themselves do not produce the androcentric views, but merely, in some cases, link to them through various steps. If one wishes to oppose androcentricity, one should reject the androcentric views themselves. The notions could be left alone.

Would I present this conclusion as universal? Is it always the case that the link would be loose, and a philosophical notion somehow linked to an androcentric claim need not be rejected or changed? I have certainly not examined all cases (although I did inspect many). Thus, there may be some exceptions, and we may yet find links that are not loose. I have not, however, found any yet.

5

Metaphors

1

Other arguments for the androcentricity of philosophy rely on claims concerning androcentric metaphors in philosophical texts. Such arguments usually take the following form:

1. Philosophy (or a certain philosophy) includes androcentric metaphors.
2. Androcentric metaphors make the philosophies containing them androcentric.
3. Conclusion: Philosophy (or a certain philosophy) is androcentric.

I will argue ahead that there are significantly fewer androcentric metaphors in philosophy than is sometimes claimed. Many presumed androcentric metaphors are not androcentric, or are not metaphors. However, I will accept that, even if less commonly than claimed, androcentric metaphors do appear in some philosophies, and that they thus make these philosophies androcentric. It remains to be examined, of course, whether they make these philosophies pervasively androcentric. In all the cases I have found, they do not.

2

A large group of claims concerning androcentric metaphors in philosophy centers on Francis Bacon's supposed use of such metaphors, especially those relating to the torture of women. Alan Soble has critiqued these arguments, showing that many of them are problematic.[1] The claim that Bacon employs such metaphors was first presented by Caroline Merchant, and has influenced many, being frequently repeated in different forms.[2] Merchant starts her discussion by discussing Bacon's patron, James I. In 1603, the king, who "supported antifeminist and antiwitchcraft legislation," changed Elizabeth I's ruling that only those who murder by witchcraft should be put to death, and instituted less tolerant laws, which imposed the death penalty for any act of witchcraft (Merchant, *Death of Nature,* 165–68). The sexual associations of witchcraft were amplified in 1612, when so-called witches were accused of fornicating with the devil (168). Merchant argues that

> these social events influenced Bacon's philosophy and literary style. Much of the imagery he used in delineating his new scientific objectives and methods derives from the courtroom, and, because it treats nature as a female to be tortured through mechanical inventions, strongly suggests the interrogations of the witch trials and the mechanical devices used to torture witches. In a relevant passage, Bacon stated that the method by which nature's secrets might be discovered consisted in investigating the secrets of witchcraft by inquisition, referring to the example of James I. (ibid.)

In support of these claims, Merchant cites the following passage from Bacon:

> *For you have but to follow and as it were hound nature in her wanderings, and you will be able when you like to lead and drive her afterward to the same place again.* Neither am I of opinion in this history of marvels that superstitious narratives of *sorceries,*

---

1. Soble, "In Defense of Bacon." My discussion of these issues in "Feminist Criticisms of Metaphors in Bacon's Philosophy of Science," *Philosophy* 73 (1998): 47–61, unknowingly repeats many of Soble's points.

2. Merchant, *Death of Nature.* Among those cited by Soble ("In Defense of Bacon," 211 n. 3) as influenced by Merchant's argument are Sandra Harding, who claims that the metaphor discusses rape (*Whose Science? Whose Knowledge?* 43, and *Science Question in Feminism,* 116). Soble points to problems in Harding's quotation of Merchant (199), as well as to some other difficulties in her account. Some other authors Soble mentions as influenced by Merchant's claim are Nelson, *Who Knows,* 213, 353 n. 136; Longino, *Science as Social Knowledge,* 3; and Agassi, "The Lark and the Tortoise," 92.

witchcrafts, charms, dreams, divinations, and the like, where there is an assurance and clear evidence of the fact, should be altogether excluded . . . howsoever the use and practice of such arts is to be condemned, yet from the speculation and consideration of them . . . a useful light may be gained, not only for a true judgement of the offenses of persons charged with such practices, but likewise for the further disclosing of the secrets of nature. Neither ought a man to make scruple of entering and penetrating into these holes and corners, when the inquisition of truth is his whole object,—as your Majesty has shown in your own example. (168; Merchant's emphases and ellipses)

Merchant adds that "the strong sexual implications of the last sentence can be interpreted in the light of the investigation of the supposed sexual crimes and practices of witches" (168–69). However, Soble shows that, even with the ellipses, the passage does not satisfactorily demonstrate Merchant's claims (Soble, "In Defense of Bacon," 203–4). It is unclear how hounding "nature in her wanderings" so that one can subsequently "lead and drive her afterwards to the same place again" is related to torturing witches with mechanical devices, or where the passage does actually employ imagery taken from the courtroom or from the torture chamber. Soble also argues that by the time Bacon's text was written, James I had changed his views concerning witches and had even intervened to save some of them from execution (204). When the sentences omitted in Merchant's citation are reinserted, it becomes clearer that Bacon is not discussing torture in this passage (ibid.). The passage then reads:

Neither am I of opinion in this history of marvels, that superstitious narrative of sorceries, witchcrafts, charms, dreams, divinations, and the like, where there is an assurance and clear evidence of the fact, should be altogether excluded. *For it is not yet known in what cases, and how far, effects attributed to superstition participate of natural causes; and therefore* howsoever the use and practice of such arts is to be condemned, yet from the speculation and consideration of them (*if they be diligently unravelled*) a useful light may be gained, not only for the true judgement of the offences of persons charged with such practices, but likewise for the further disclosing of the secrets of nature.[3]

3. Soble, "In Defense of Bacon," 204; italics indicate the reinserted sentences.

Bacon is simply suggesting here, then, that views issuing from sorceries and witchcraft should not be automatically rejected; they should rather be seriously considered, since they may have perfectly natural explanations. Bacon further suggests that a more careful consideration of them may throw light on natural events and enhance our knowledge.

Merchant also argues that Bacon "pressed the idea further with an analogy to the torture chamber" (*Death of Nature,* 169), citing the following:

> For like as a man's disposition is never well known or proved till he be crossed, nor Proteus ever changed shapes till he was *straitened* and *held fast,* so nature exhibits herself more clearly under the *trials* and *vexations* of art [mechanical devices] than when left to herself. (Merchant's emphases)

Soble shows, however, that nature is compared here not to a woman but to a man, and then to Proteus, a male mythological creature who knew everything, but was reluctant to share his knowledge. Those who wished to confer with him had to bind him during his sleep. He would try to change his form and escape, but if held firmly for some time would eventually return to his original shape and answer the questions posed to him.[4] The point of the citation is that "we must be smart enough to outfox nature to get a hearing for our questions. . . . Our attempts to bind her will be largely fruitless" (Soble, "In Defense of Bacon," 204–5). Soble also points out that Bacon uses the verb "to bind" in a variety of contexts, many of them unrelated to nature, and some of them favorable. Moreover, for Bacon, human constraint of nature need not be violent or torturing (209–10).

3

Another large group of such claims centers on visual metaphors—knowledge as light, knowing as seeing, and so on. Alessandra Tanesini, for example, writes that "in order to understand what 'objectivity' may mean we need to consider the influence of metaphors of vision on theories of knowledge."[5] She discusses in this context two visual metaphors. In

4. *Odyssey* 4.382–460.
5. *Introduction to Feminist Epistemologies,* 161.

the first "vision is understood as the power of the eye to represent the world as it is." In the second "vision is conceived as an asymmetrical relation between an active eye and a passive object. Through vision the object is objectified: that is, it comes to be seen as devoid of meaning or purpose" (161). Tanesini believes that "these two metaphors of sight are at the root of the conception of knowledge as adequate representation. The traditional problem of objectivity . . . makes sense only in the context of this conception" (162). Likewise, in her 1987 essay "Feminism, Marxism, Method, and the State: Toward Feminist Jurisprudence," Catharine MacKinnon writes that

> at least since Plato's cave, visual metaphors for knowing have been central to Western theories of knowledge, the visual sense prioritized as a mode of verification. The relationship between visual appropriation and objectification is now only beginning to be explored. "The knowledge gained through still photographs will always be . . . a semblance of knowledge, a semblance of wisdom, as the act of taking pictures is a semblance of wisdom, a semblance of rape. The very muteness of what is, hypothetically, comprehensible in photographs is what constitutes their attraction and provocativeness" (Susan Sontag, *On Photography* [New York: 1980] p. 24).[6]

MacKinnnon qualifies her claim, stating that "the relationship between visual appropriation and objectification is now only beginning to be explored," which suggests that she is not certain about the extent to which the relation indeed holds. In her later work *Toward a Feminist Theory of the State,* she writes about the issue in stronger terms: "At least since Plato's cave, this appropriation has been achieved first visually, visual metaphors for knowing have been prioritized as a method of verification, giving visual objectification, as in pornography, particular potency."[7]

Lorraine Code, too, takes visual metaphors to be androcentric when she writes that "vision is the privileged sense in the construction of this subject-object relation. Visual metaphors—knowledge as illumination, knowledge as seeing, truth as light—shape hegemonic conceptions of knowledge just as surely as masculine metaphors shape hegemonic con-

---

6. "Feminism, Marxism, Method, and the State: Toward Feminist Jurisprudence," 150 n. 4; MacKinnon's ellipsis.
    7. *Toward a Feminist Theory of the State,* 114–15.

ceptions of reason."[8] Since here she is linking visual metaphors to the scientific model and "the autonomy-of-reason credo," and earlier (*What Can She Know?* 53–54, 121) she links the scientific model and "the autonomy-of-reason credo" to masculinity, visual metaphors appear to be connected to masculinity for her. Code also writes that "there are convergences between my project and certain aspects of these philosophers' [Heidegger and Merleau-Ponty] thought, convergences that open possibilities of dialogue between feminists who take issue with the dominant epistemological discourse, and phenomenologists" (148). One of these convergences is that Heidegger and Merleau-Ponty "do not privilege vision; perception engages all of the senses" (ibid.). It is not completely clear, however, how Code's view on this subject should be understood, since her text includes also some indications that suggest that she does *not* in fact take visual metaphors to be androcentric.[9] The following discussion assumes that she does; if she does not, I have no disagreement with her.

The visual metaphor arguments are not entirely clear. MacKinnon's, and perhaps Tanesini's, may rely on the fact that vision is sometimes used in an objectifying manner, especially in cases of pornographic objectification (MacKinnon alludes to such cases, although it is not clear that she intends this to be an argument for the androcentricity of visual metaphors in general). While I accept that there are cases of visual objectification, this, of course, is not a sufficient basis for arguing that all visual experiences are objectifying. I also accept that some visual metaphors are androcentric (although I do not see how Plato's Cave, which MacKinnon mentions in this context, relates to visual appropriation or objectifica-

---

8. *What Can She Know?* 140.

9. This is because Code also points out that there is more than one way to understand vision. Following Fox Keller and Grontkowski, "Mind's Eye," she claims that vision also functions through direct eye contact as "a symmetrical act of mutual recognition in which neither need be passive and neither in control. . . . Through it . . . [people] engage with one another, convey feelings, and establish and maintain, or re-negotiate, their relationships. . . . This . . . is a model . . . for the communicative and connective (as contrasted with the distancing, objectifying) aspects of vision." *What Can She Know?* 144–45. This appears to be in conflict with the claims that visual metaphors are related to a manipulating, predicting, and controlling subject-object relation (144), and that feminists who take issue with the dominant epistemological discourse should turn to Heidegger and Merleau-Ponty, whose philosophies do not privilege sight (148–49). Perhaps, then, Code believes that although sight and visual metaphors have both a connective and a divisive character, their connective character is weaker than the connective character of hearing or other senses, or that vision's divisive character is stronger than that of other senses. It is difficult to think of any other way of reading her text. The following discussion is based on this understanding of Code's view.

tion).[10] But of course, acknowledging the existence of a few androcentric visual metaphors is hardly sufficient evidence that all visual metaphors are androcentric (again, it is possible that MacKinnon and Tanesini are not making this argument).

Code's argument and perhaps part of Tanesini's seem to follow a different route. The argument focuses on some epistemic standards or ideals in Western philosophy, such as atemporality, lack of involvement with action or experience, disengagement from interaction, distance between the sensing subject and the sensed object, being less or non-body bound, noncontingency, and objectivity. These standards are taken to be androcentric, and it is suggested that Western philosophy has been influenced toward them by visual metaphors, since atemporality, lack of involvement, and so on, are also the characteristics of sight. However, even if it is granted, for the sake of argument, that these standards or ideals are indeed androcentric, the argument seems problematic. Much of philosophy is *not* typified by these epistemic standards. The argument discussed here would be stronger if, in those parts of philosophy where these standards do not appear, there were no, or fewer, visual metaphors. However, this is not the case. When we examine the actual use of visual metaphors in the history of philosophy, we see that they frequently have been used to describe *not* what is taken to be disengaged, nonexperiential, and noninteractive logical-objectivist knowledge of the type described in the arguments above, but rather engaged, interactive, dynamic, and experiential religious knowledge, described in many theological writings, and frequently even nonobjectivist, immediate, mystical-experiential understanding (as, for example, in Plato, Plotinus, Proclus, and Philo).[11]

Visual metaphors are popular, I suggest, not because of any special relation to objectivist, disengaged knowledge, but because in humans

10. Perhaps MacKinnon takes the cave to be a metaphor of the womb, and the effort to leave it as a metaphor for rejecting femininity. If this is so, however, the claim concerning (visual) appropriation or objectification is unclear. I discuss Phyllis Rooney's explicit presentation of the analogy between the cave and a womb in section 4.

11. See Plato Letter 7, 341c; Plotinus *Enneads* 5.1, 6; Proclus *Platonic Theology* 1.14 (*Théologie Platonicienne*, edited and translated by H. D. Saffrey and L. G. Westerink [Paris: Les Belles Lettres, 1968], 67); and Philo *On Drunkenness* 43–44. See also Augustine *Confessions* 8.29 and 9.1. Visual metaphors are prevalent also in many other non-logical-objectivist contexts, such as German Idealism. See, for example, Johann Gottlieb Fichte, "The Nature of the Scholar," in *The Popular Works of Johann Gottlieb Fichte*, trans. William Smith (London: Trübner, 1889; reprint, Bristol: Thoemmes, 1999), 1:317, and "The Vocation of Man," ibid., 478. Also see Friedrich Wilhelm Joseph Schelling, *Bruno, or On the Natural and the Divine Principle of Things*, trans. Michael G. Vater (Albany: SUNY Press, 1984), 222–23.

(unlike, for example, canines, felines, and many other animals), sight is more developed than the other senses, and thus is more helpful in finding our way about the world.[12] It is because of this that philosophers who wanted to describe knowledge in a metaphorical way chose metaphors of sight rather than, say, of smell. They used visual metaphors to describe the type of knowledge that seemed to them to be superior. Some employed visual metaphors to describe logical-objectivist knowledge, and others, many in number, used visual metaphors to describe spiritual or religious knowledge, or even immediate, experiential-mystical knowledge.

Nor is it correct to suggest, as Code's argument does, that atemporality, noncontingency, and all the other characteristics claimed to be androcentric, are typical of sight more than of touch (which Code underscores) or the other senses. Take atemporality: vision is no more atemporal than other senses, including touch.[13] When what is seen, or touched, is unchanging (for example, a brick on the table), the sensation it imparts is atemporal. When what is experienced is changing (for example, a moving animal), the sensation it imparts is temporal. The same is true of the claim concerning "disengagement from action, experience, and dynamic interaction" (ibid.). Vision is not more disengaged from experiencing the world, from dynamic interactions, and from actions, than are touch and other senses; when we act, experience, or interact, we can touch things, see things, smell things, and so on, and I do not see why employing one

12. Code suggests that it is not the case that, in humans, sight is more developed than the other senses, and thus is more helpful in finding our way about the world: "Touch is a source of knowledge at once more detailed and more stable than vision. With tactile confirmation, people are more secure in trusting their visual perceptions." *What Can She Know?* 149. I have to disagree. It seems that most people, most of the time, receive more detailed and reliable information about most objects through sight than through touch. Code is right, of course, in pointing out that in many cases where only visual perceptions are offered, added tactile information increases reliability and detail. But the opposite is equally true: when only tactile information is offered, added visual perceptions also increase reliability and detail.

13. For Code's discussion of vision and atemporality, see *What Can She Know?* 141–42. Code cites a passage from Fox Keller and Grontkowski, "Mind's Eye," 219–20. (Note, however, that Fox Keller and Grontkowski discuss the *apparent* atemporality of sight.) Notwithstanding this and other passages in their article, Fox Keller and Grontkowski conclude that the use of the visual metaphor in Western philosophy is too varied to allow the inference that it is androcentric (220–21). According to my understanding of Code, she takes Fox Keller and Grontkowski's conclusion to be too weak, and employs some of their arguments to support a more radical thesis than theirs. Although some of the following critiques are relevant also to Fox Keller and Grontkowski's work, they are presented here only with reference to Code.

of these senses would be more disengaged than employing another. Thus, even if it is granted, for the sake of argument, that these characteristics are androcentric, sight is on a par, in this respect too, with touch (as well as with taste, hearing, and smell).

It may be replied, however, that sight, more than touch, allows distance between the sensing subject and the sensed object (ibid.), and that sight is less body bound than touch (ibid.). I agree that these characteristics are true of sight (especially in comparison with touch and taste, although less so, or not at all, in comparison with smell or hearing), so that if these characteristics are related to androcentricity, sight would be more androcentric in these respects. But Code also suggests that sight is less related to contingency than other senses (ibid.). Here, it seems, the opposite is the case: when we move from daylight into a dark place it takes time for our vision to adjust; then when we go back outside, we again need time to get used to daylight. When exposed to glaring light we are temporarily blinded. Square, flat surfaces look like rectangles from one perspective, parallelograms from another, and thin lines from a third; and at sunset, noon and dusk objects seem to have different colors. It seems, then, that we have a wider and more flexible variety of visual experiences among which it is not always easy to decide which is the more "correct," than we have of tactile experiences. Thus it would appear that vision is the *least* likely model for what might be taken to be an "objectivist" understanding of the world, according to which we can know it "as it really is." If "noncontingency" is taken to partly constitute androcentricity, touch, rather than sight, should be considered androcentric.

The same is true of another characteristic; Code argues (basing the contention to some extent on Sartre and Foucault) that vision is a better means of surveillance than are other senses, and as a result of this connection to surveillance, she relates vision also to objectification and control (142–44). However, vision does not seem to be more functional for objectification and control than is touch. As can unhappily be verified time and again by Amnesty International reports, it is by the latter sense that people are subjected to extreme control and objectification. In this respect, too, then, if the presuppositions of the argument are accepted, it seems that touch, rather than sight, should be implicated. All in all, then, it is not clear that sight has more "androcentric" characteristics than touch or other senses, even if the androcentric quality of all these characteristics is accepted. These difficulties, I believe, suggest that the argument

for the androcentricity of visual metaphors, and their effect on the androcentricity of Western philosophy, should not be accepted.

4

Many other arguments concerning androcentric metaphors do not fall
into specific groups or genres. For example, Catharine MacKinnon argues that

> sexual metaphors for knowing are no coincidence. In the Bible,
> to know a woman is to have sex with her. You acquire carnal
> knowledge. Many scholarly metaphors elaborate the theme of
> violating boundaries to appropriate from inside to carry off, the
> classic meaning of rape. [Endnote:] One often hears of "a pene-
> trating observation," "an incisive analysis," "piercing the
> veil."[14]

These claims too seem to me problematic. I will not discuss here in detail
the claim about biblical Hebrew, since it does not directly relate to philosophy.[15] I suggest, however, that "piercing the veil" is no more than a
simple metaphor for something that, falling between an object and ourselves, hinders our ability to see it. When the veil is pierced, the impedi-
ment is cleared away. Incisiveness is an epithet for something that dissects
or separates parts of a compound whole. "Penetrating observation" sig-
nifies that the examination relates not only to the superficial and external
aspects of a certain issue, but also to the deeper ones ("superficial," "external," and "deep" are, of course, also metaphors, all belonging to the
same—asexual—family). I agree that these metaphors *may* also be seen

---

14. *Toward a Feminist Theory of the State,* 114, 273 n. 27.

15. However, it should be pointed out that the verb *yada* in biblical Hebrew has meanings beyond those of "to know" and "to have sexual intercourse." Among other meanings,
yada means also "to appreciate or discern favorably" (Hos. 5:3; Amos 3:2); "to take an
interest in or care for" (Gen. 39:6, 8); and "to recognize or accept" (Exod. 5:2). The root
of the verb is used also to indicate family kinship (Ruth 2:1). All these are different meanings of the same word, and none seems to be a metaphor of others. However, if there is a
case for asserting some common denominator for these meanings, it probably has to do
with familiarity or connection. It should be noted also that as a sexual term, the verb is
used to denote in some cases mere intercourse (Gen. 4:1; 38:26), in others rape and torture
(Judg. 19:22, 25), and in yet others intercourse related to love (1 Sam. 1:1–20, esp. 5, 8,
19). Men can "know" women, and women can also "know" men (Gen. 19:8; Num. 31:17,
18, 35; Judg. 11:39; 21:11, 12).

as sexual, but I think it is unlikely that those who have used them, or those who have been exposed to them, had any sexual connotations in mind. I suggest, moreover, that even if it is accepted that these metaphors and expressions are sexual, the first and last do not thereby become androcentric. True, if incisiveness is sexual, then indeed it is related to violent and probably involuntary sexual intercourse, and is thus sexist. But the two other examples—"piercing the veil" and "penetrating observation"—do not provide sufficient evidence that they represent violation of boundaries, appropriation from inside, carrying off, or rape.

Another argument discusses Plato's Cave and Socrates' midwifery metaphor. While, as we have seen above, MacKinnon relates the Cave to sight, Phyllis Rooney, following Luce Irigaray, takes it to be a metaphor of the womb.[16] I understand, of course, how similarity can be found between a cave and a womb. But I doubt that Plato's Cave should be understood as alluding to the womb or femininity, since so much in the metaphor—from the prisoners, the figures that the prisoners cannot see, the people who move around carrying those figures, the fire inside, its pale light, the shadows and images reflected on the wall, the honors the prisoners confer among themselves for their familiarity with the shadows, to the philosopher's decision to return to the cave in order to save the other prisoners—is completely unrelated to such issues. It may be answered, of course, that leaving the cave for the daylight can be seen as rejection of the womb, and hence of femininity. If, notwithstanding the reservations noted above, the cave is still seen as a womb, then this indeed is one possible way of understanding this metaphor. But it seems just as plausible to interpret leaving it on the way to true knowledge as a metaphor of birth rather than of a rejection of womanhood. Thus, it would be a feminine-oriented rather than an androcentric metaphor. Socrates' midwifery metaphor also seems feminine-oriented rather than androcentric.

Rooney, who takes the cave metaphor to be androcentric, presents it and the midwifery metaphor as linked, and, following Fox Keller, takes this to be an example of a psychological Oedipal structure, where boys are ambivalent about the feminine element, feeling the wish to both deny and appropriate it. She writes:

> Plato's *Theaetetus* metaphor of the philosopher of ideas as a *midwife* may seem to reverse the gender orientation of the cre-

16. "Gendered Reason," 80. Rooney relies on Irigaray's discussion in *Speculum of the Other Woman*, 243.

ator, the generator, the arbiter of ideas and truth. Yet we should notice that Socrates is presenting *himself* as the midwife ministering to Theaetetus's philosophical confusions. . . . Juxtaposing the allegory of the cave with the image of the philosopher as midwife gives a fairly compelling picture of a drawing away from the realm of the maternal and the female in what is surely another paradigm example of the "simultaneous appropriation and denial of the feminine."[17]

I believe, however, that linking the two metaphors is problematic, since the cave metaphor appears in the *Republic,* whereas the midwifery metaphor figures in a very different context, in the *Theaetetus.* It is thus unlikely that they are two parts of the same structure.

5

Although the number of androcentric metaphors in philosophy is significantly smaller than it is frequently argued to be, some androcentric metaphors are to be found in various philosophical texts. Sandra Harding, for example, presents an example from Paul Feyerabend's philosophy of science:

Paul Feyerabend, a contemporary philosopher of science, has recommended his own analysis over competing ones by saying that "such a development . . . changes science from a stern and demanding mistress into an attractive and yielding courtesan who tries to anticipate every wish of her lover. Of course it is up to us to choose either a dragon or a pussy cat for our company. I think I do not have to explain my own preferences."[18]

Likewise, Rooney presents an example of an androcentric metaphor in Locke:

17. "Gendered Reason," 80; Rooney's emphases. The quotation is from Fox Keller, *Reflections on Gender and Science,* 41.
18. *Whose Science? Whose Knowledge?* 43; Harding's ellipses. Feyerabend tries to defend himself from a somewhat similar criticism by Hilary Rose in his *Killing Time,* 148–50. Soble argues that Feyerabend "conceived of women only as kittens or stern mistresses, imagery that excessively narrows women's modes of existence," and that this is true also of Bacon's imagery. "In Defense of Bacon," 209.

All the art of rhetorick, besides order and clearness, all the arti-
ficial and figurative application of words eloquence hath in-
vented, are for nothing else but to insinuate wrong ideas, move
the passions, and thereby mislead the judgment . . . *eloquence,*
like the fair sex, has too prevailing beauties in it to suffer itself
ever to be spoken against. And it is vain to find fault with those
arts of deceiving wherein men find pleasure to be deceived.[19]

Rooney also cites Aristotle's "there is a justice, not indeed between a
man and himself, but between certain parts of him; yet not every kind of
justice but that of master and servant or that of husband and wife. For
these are the ratios in which the part of the soul that has a rational principle stands to the irrational part . . . there is therefore thought to be a
mutual justice between them [the parts of the soul] as between ruler and
ruled."[20] Other androcentric metaphors, represented by Rooney ("Gendered Reason," 82), can be found in, among others, Philo, Augustine,
and Aquinas, who all compare to men what they take to be the higher
human functions (for example, reason), and compare to women what
they take to be the lower functions (for example, sense). And I am sure
that there are other philosophical texts that include some androcentric
metaphors. As claimed in section 1, such androcentric metaphors make
the philosophies in which they appear androcentric. But do they make
the philosophies also pervasively androcentric? Does rejecting the androcentric metaphors require rejecting as well other parts of the theories in
which these metaphors appear?

An androcentric metaphor may be related to other parts of the theory
in which it appears, so that rejecting it requires also rejecting them, in
two main ways. First, the androcentric metaphor may affect views expressed in the theory, making them, too, androcentric. In such a case we
would have, of course, to reject as androcentric not only the metaphor
but also these views. Second, even if the androcentric metaphor does not
make the views expressed in the theory androcentric, it may be so cohesively linked with them that rejecting the metaphor requires rejecting the
views as well. The former and latter cases may, but do not have to, coin-

19. Locke, *Essay Concerning Human Understanding,* bk. 3, chap. 10, sec. 34; quoted
in Rooney, "Gendered Reason," 84; Rooney's ellipses. Rooney's quotation is slightly inac-
curate; the emphasis on "eloquence" is hers, not his, and he writes that "it is in vain to find
faults" rather than that "it is vain to find faults." But these inaccuracies are inconsequential
here.

20. *Nicomachean Ethics* V 11 1138b5–13; Rooney, "Gendered Reason," 81.

cide: an androcentric metaphor may both be cohesively linked with views expressed in the theory, and affect them into being androcentric. But a metaphor may also be cohesively linked with views expressed in the theory without making them androcentric.

Rooney suggests that many, or perhaps all, metaphors do affect the content of the theories in which they appear. Thus, she writes that "it would be very difficult to argue for a view of metaphor as simply 'stylistic embellishment,' given the analysis of metaphor—philosophical and literary—during the last fifty years or so. There is a general agreement that metaphor contributes in some way to content and argumentation in philosophical and scientific discourse, though there has been some disagreement about what form that contribution takes" (86). I suggest, however, that there is no general agreement that metaphor contributes to the content and argumentation of philosophical discourse; it is commonly accepted that some metaphors contribute to content and argumentation, and others do not. Each should be examined on its own.

Rooney elaborates on two theories of metaphor: the traditionally accepted substitution (or comparison) theory of metaphor, and the modern interactionist theory of metaphor, which was suggested by Max Black in reaction to the substitution theory.[21] According to the substitution theory, a metaphor is based on a comparison of two terms ("topic" and "vehicle" in the traditional terminology, "principal subject" and "subsidiary subject" in Black's) that bear a partial resemblance to each other. To understand a metaphor the interpreter compares the two terms and finds the relevant shared properties. Once the metaphor is understood, it can be replaced by its meaning. To take a standard example, if Richard is metaphorically referred to as a lion, the interpreter compares "Richard" and "lion" and finds the relevant shared properties (such as courage and strength). Once this has been done, the metaphor "lion" can be replaced with its meaning. According to Black's interactionist theory, however, rather than highlighting unnoticed but previously existing properties, both principal and subsidiary subjects interact so that the meaning of both is changed, thus creating new connotations and frameworks of meaning that cannot be reduced to literal ones. Hence, at least some metaphors are untranslatable and cannot be replaced by alternative notions and terms. Another important interactionist, Mary Hesse, uses Black's work to develop the "network" theory of metaphors, and employs it in, among others, her philosophy of science. Unlike Black, Hesse takes all

21. See Black, "Metaphor" and "More about Metaphor."

language to be metaphorical, and sees the distinction between the metaphoric and literal as pragmatic, not semantic. Moreover, while Black's theory refrains from discussing similarities between the "principal subject" and "subsidiary subject," Hesse's network theory depends on them. Hesse also emphasizes that metaphors are the basis of new hypotheses and predictions, and thus are central to scientific progress.[22]

Thus, according to interactionism and the network theory, androcentric metaphors can affect the content of the theories in which they appear. Moreover, the relation between androcentric metaphors and the content can be more cohesive than it may at first seem; it may not be possible to replace the androcentric metaphors with nonandrocentric terms. This means that androcentric metaphors may render the philosophies in which they appear pervasively androcentric, since, at least in some cases, we could not reject the metaphors without rejecting also that part of the content that is androcentrically affected by or cohesively linked with the metaphor.

Interactionists and network theorists, however, rarely believe that *all* metaphors affect the content of the theories in which they are found. Hesse, for example, does not think that all metaphors are explanatory and significant for scientific theories, or that all are a substantive part of science and show scientists how to extend the domains of their theories. Thus, although Hesse accepts that metaphors are necessary for the progress of science, she does not claim that each and every metaphor is influential; she believes that there cannot be scientific progress without metaphors, but not that there cannot be metaphors without influence on the scientific progress. She asserts, rather, that the "introduction of a metaphoric terminology is not in itself explanatory," and that "the connection between metaphor and explanation is . . . neither that of necessary nor sufficient condition. Metaphor becomes explanatory only when it satisfies certain further conditions."[23]

Note also that an androcentric metaphor may affect the content of a theory without making the content *androcentric*. This is because the androcentric elements in the metaphor may not be relevant and significant to the role that the metaphor plays in the theory. Not *all* the aspects or connotations of a metaphor play a part when it is employed. For ex-

---

22. See Hesse, *Models and Analogies in Science* and "Cognitive Claims of Metaphor." Especially in the first of these texts, Hesse focuses on science rather than on philosophy, but it seems that she would apply her theory to philosophical texts as well.

23. *Models and Analogies in Science,* 171.

ample, in the metaphor "John is a cold fish," the speaker is not suggesting that John has gills or lives in water.

Moreover, according to interactionism, a metaphor may be androcentric, affect *with its androcentric elements* the content of the theory, and yet not transform the content of the theory into being androcentric but, on the contrary, have the metaphor's androcentric meaning moderated or transformed. This is because the androcentric connotations of the androcentric elements may change when the metaphor is put to work. As recounted—but insufficiently noted, I believe—by Rooney herself ("Gendered Reason," 87), according to Black's interactionism, when the principal and subsidiary subjects interact with each other, the initial meanings of *both* subjects change.[24] Hence, neither should be understood verbatim. Hesse too argues that "for a conjunction of terms . . . to constitute a metaphor, it is necessary that there should be a patent falsehood or even absurdity in taking the conjunction literally."[25] Again, then, although androcentric metaphors may make the content of the theories in which they appear androcentric, they do not have to do so. Each case should be examined individually.

Of course, androcentric metaphors may not make the content of the theories in which they appear androcentric, but still be so cohesively related to the content that rejecting them requires rejecting the content also. But as before, although metaphors and content may be related in this way, they do not have to be. Black, for example, holds that there are interactive metaphors on the one hand, and substitution metaphors on the other. Whereas the former cannot be replaced by literal translations, the latter can, "by sacrificing some of the charm, vivacity, or wit of the original, but with no loss of *cognitive* content."[26] Again, then, there may be cases where we can reject an androcentric metaphor without also having to reject any part of the content of the theory in which the metaphor appears.

Rooney also discusses the substitution theory, and suggests that under this theory, too, metaphors can be understood as influencing the content of philosophy, since they function as arguments by analogy ("Gendered Reason," 86).[27] But substitution theorists, too, do not think that all meta-

24. Black, "Metaphor," 38–40, 45; Black, "More About Metaphor," 29.
25. *Models and Analogies in Science*, 74. See also "Cognitive Claims of Metaphor," 4.
26. "Metaphor," 46; Black's emphasis.
27. Rooney is not entirely clear on whether she takes all metaphors, when understood according to the substitution theory, to influence content. This is because of the possible tension between her claim that "such an analysis might fit a few of our examples above" ("Gendered Reason," 86), which suggests that the substitution analysis does not suits all

phors affect content. Traditional substitutionalists have frequently taken metaphors to function as mere embellishments, and modern substitutionalists, who present stronger and more sophisticated versions of the theory, frequently point out the wide variety of types of metaphor. Thus Susan Haack, for example, suggests neither that all metaphors are merely ornamental or heuristic devices, nor that all affect the content of the philosophy in which they appear. Haack emphasizes that metaphors come in many versions and types, and takes some of them to be helpful for inquiry, others to be harmless, and yet others to be a hindrance to it. Some are substantial to the theories in which they appear, others are not.[28]

The same is true for authors who are neither interactionists nor substitutionalists. Donald Davidson, for example, rejects altogether the notion of metaphorical meaning and its difference from literal meaning. Instead he emphasizes the effect that metaphors have on their audience.[29] John Searle distinguishes between "word or sentence meaning" and "speaker's utterance meaning," and provides various principles by which hearers can understand the latter.[30] Searle's and Davidson's theories, too, allow that some metaphors are ornamental, others are heuristic devices, and yet others are substantive to theories and related research. Modern theories of metaphor, then, suggest that it is possible, but not necessary, that metaphors affect or cohesively relate to the content or argument of theories.

To determine the place of a certain metaphor in a philosophy we should examine, of course, not only whether it influences or cohesively interrelates with the content of the philosophy, but also—as Soble and Haack contend—the extent of its influence or interrelatedness.[31] We should examine, among other issues, which parts of the argument or content of the philosophy the metaphor influences or interrelates with, and their place in the philosophy at large. Thus, even in cases where part

---

cases, and her claim that "there is a general agreement that metaphor contributes in some way to the content and argumentation in philosophical and scientific discourse, though there has been some disagreement about what form that contribution makes" (ibid.). Rooney probably means that not all metaphors can be made sense of by the substitution theory, but all those that can do contribute to content and argumentation.

28. "Dry Truth and Real Knowledge," 72, 84.
29. See Davidson, "What Metaphors Mean."
30. See Searle, "Metaphor," esp. 113–23.
31. Soble, "In Defense of Bacon," 208; Haack, "Science as Social?—Yes and No," 117. Soble presents a full list of the necessary conditions that need to be satisfied in order to show that Bacon intentionally used torture or rape metaphors to persuade his readers to accept the experimental method.

of the content of the theory is affected androcentrically or is cohesively interrelated with the androcentric metaphor, the theory may not be pervasively androcentric, since the affected or interrelated part may not be important or central to the theory as a whole.

The discussion suggests, then, that we should not generalize about metaphors, but examine each individually. Metaphors may or may not be androcentric; they may or may not affect, or be cohesively interrelated with, parts of the theories in which they appear; and these parts may or may not be central or important in those theories. We have to inspect each case on its own.

6

Let us examine, then, some of the androcentric metaphors mentioned above. Take, for example, Locke's view concerning eloquence, and the metaphor he uses in this context. One should point out the androcentric connotations of the metaphor. But should Locke's view concerning eloquence (or wider parts of his philosophy) be rejected as well? We should consider, first, whether the metaphor affects the view into being androcentric. Is the view that eloquence is pleasantly deceptive androcentric? We may or may not reject the view as wrong (I do not think that eloquence is always deceptive), but I do not see anything androcentric in the view itself. (It may be suggested that the view is androcentric because some will *associate* eloquence with women; but this type of argument, which I discussed in Chapter 3 is different from the type examined here.) The androcentric metaphor, then, does not make Locke's views on eloquence androcentric.

We should consider, next, whether the androcentric metaphor is linked to the view in such a way that one cannot reject the metaphor without rejecting also the view. Is there such a cohesive link between the two? The answer again is negative. The view can be easily expressed in literal terms (and Locke indeed does so). From this respect too, then, we can reject this androcentric metaphor without changing anything else in the system. (Note also that even if it were the case that Locke's view concerning eloquence had to be rejected, this would have not made much difference in Locke's theory as a whole.) Locke's androcentric metaphor, then, makes his philosophy only nonpervasively androcentric.

Consider, similarly, Philo's analogy between the hierarchy he believes to exist between women and men, on the one hand, and the hierarchy he believes to exist between mind and sense, on the other. One should, of course, reject the androcentric metaphor. But since Philo's view about the value of mind and sense is not in itself androcentric, we have another example where the androcentric metaphor does not make the content of the theory andocentric. One may, of course, have various other reasons for accepting or rejecting Philo's view about the value of mind and sense. But the view does not, in itself, lead to the domination of women by men, involve male discrimination against women, or suit men's experiences or minds more than women's.[32]

Perhaps, however, although the androcentric metaphor does not make the view androcentric, it is cohesively linked to the view to such an extent that one cannot reject the metaphor without rejecting also the view. Again, this does not seem to be the case. The view does not depend on the metaphor, and one can express, understand, argue for, or accept the view without even thinking of the metaphor. Rejecting the metaphor, then, does not require rejecting the view as well. This androcentric metaphor, too, renders the philosophy only nonpervasively androcentric. The same is true of the other metaphors mentioned, such as Aristotle's claims concerning the rational and irrational parts of the soul, and the metaphor he uses about the relation between husband and wife.

These suggestions are at odds with Rooney's, who takes the androcentric metaphors to relate to each other ("Gendered Reason," 89–94), and relies also on arguments from explicit androcentric claims and arguments from associations (already considered in Chapters 2 and 3; this chapter discusses only Rooney's arguments from metaphors). From some philosophers' employment of sexist metaphors, and claims about men's rationality and women's materiality or emotionality, Rooney concludes that this is a model, in other words, a "sustained and systematic use of a metaphor" (88). Every philosopher who prefers intellect to emotion, or mind over matter, is taken also to prefer men to women, or masculinity to femininity:

> The path of reason, the path to knowledge and truth, will involve in some way a transcendence of the "feminine." The words "female" or "feminine" need not be used. We may simply get a discussion about the need to control the irrational impulses, instincts, "lower" passions, or the vagaries of nature. Yet the

32. Again, some may claim that there are androcentric associations to this view, but this is a different type of argument, which I discussed in Chapter 3.

> imaginative and emotional substructure that makes such needs
> seem self-evident is often revealed quite surprisingly in an overt
> preference, or in the workings of what may seem like a super-
> fluous metaphor. (80)

Moreover,

> this sex metaphor structure operates in at least facilitating the
> view that the contents of mind or consciousness can be neatly
> partitioned into various groupings—beliefs, thoughts, desires,
> feelings, instinct, and so on. More significantly, it helps animate
> the image of a type of *great divide*: constellated around reason
> on one side we have understanding, a properly disciplined will,
> rational beliefs, and so on; and constellated around unreason on
> the other side are feelings (especially irrational ones), impulses,
> imaginings, dreams, and intuitions. (92; Rooney's emphasis)

However, no evidence is presented for the claim that sex metaphors
significantly facilitated the acceptance of these views. Nor are the metaphors needed for this purpose, since there are many other, *prima facie*
acceptable philosophical and practical reasons for holding these views,
which appear in many philosophical works where the metaphor is not
present. The absence of this metaphor in philosophical works where such
views are held may be more common than its occurrence. (Note, moreover, that an androcentric metaphor that facilitates the acceptance of a
certain view or animates an image need not make that view or image
androcentric.)

In Rooney's argument, however, the metaphor also taints as androcentric discussions where it is not present, since they too are taken to be
instances of what Rooney terms "the great divide" (between women, passivity, sense, and so on, on the one hand, and men, activity, reason, and
so on, on the other), or of the transcendence of the feminine. This allows
Rooney to find androcentricity where, I believe, it does not exist. For
example, she argues (following Annette Baier) that Donald Davidson's
analysis of akratic action is intellectualist (93).[33] Davidson assumes that
deliberative reason (rather than, say, impulses and emotions) can and
should control human action, and thus finds it philosophically puzzling
when this does not happen. Baier, who discusses Davidson's view, em-

---

33. Davidson, "Paradoxes of Irrationality"; Baier, "Rhyme and Reason."

ploys the metaphor of "governor" and "rebellious subjects." However, referring to this metaphor—which appears in Baier's text, not in Davidson's—Rooney argues, concerning Davidson's analysis, that

> sovereign reason's political, gender, and class affiliations need to be examined more expressly. How does the image of separable male ruler exerting sovereign authority over his unruly "feminine" subject inform persistent, unconscious views of reason as ideally separable from and exerting control of the more "feminine" element of the psyche? The imaginative pull of certain male ideal of social arrangements are surely not far from the surface here also. (93)

I find it difficult to accept this argument. As I have suggested above, there are many cases where metaphors are not androcentric. Moreover, where they are, they may or may not affect or be cohesively linked to the content of the theories in which they appear. Extrapolating from cases where metaphors are androcentric (or affect content, or are linked to it) to cases where they are not is as legitimate as extrapolating in the opposite direction. It does not seem that the metaphor shows the view or theory in question to be androcentric, much less pervasively androcentric.

What has been suggested here concerning Locke's, Philo's, or Aristotle's metaphors is true of every other androcentric metaphor I have up to now found in philosophy. None makes the views in the philosophies androcentric, and none is cohesively linked with the views. Thus, they do not make the philosophies in which they appear pervasively androcentric. Of course, such androcentric metaphors might still be found. At present, however, it seems that we should accept that there are androcentric metaphors in some philosophical theories, and that they make these philosophies nonpervasively androcentric, but no more than that.

6

Values, Interests, and Domination

Another group of arguments for the androcentricity of philosophy, more often heard than read, emphasizes interests and values and discusses the influence of the gender of the authors, or that of the genderedness of the social reality in which the philosophy was composed, on the philosophy.[1] Some such arguments start out with the claim that philosophy has been almost exclusively authored by men. They can be presented thus:

1. Philosophy has been almost exclusively authored by men.
2. Philosophy reflects the interests and values of its authors.
3. Women's and men's interests and values differ.
4. Conclusion: Philosophy reflects the interests and values of men; that is, philosophy is androcentric.[2]

In other cases the arguments take a somewhat different form, and start out with the claim that philosophy reflects the interests and values of the culture or social reality in which it is composed. This type of argument can be presented thus:

1. The term "interest" is, of course, used here in the sense related to profit or advantage, rather than in the sense of intellectual curiosity. I sometimes use "interests" and "values" interchangeably. This does not affect my argument.

2. The shorter argument, that philosophy must be androcentric because it was almost entirely written by men, is frequently shorthand for the type of arguments examined here. As Jean Grimshaw points out regarding this abbreviated argument, philosophy has, indeed, been almost entirely written by men, "but it does not follow from this *alone* that philosophical theories can be seen as male in any interesting sense; that if women had done more philosophy they would have done it differently; that any sort of distinctively male perspective or viewpoint can be identified." Grimshaw, *Philosophy and Feminist Thinking*, 36; Grimshaw's emphasis.

1. Philosophy reflects the interests and values of the culture or social reality in which it is composed.
2. The interests and values of the culture or social reality in which philosophy has been composed are androcentric.
3. Conclusion: Philosophy is androcentric.

In yet other cases the argument is represented in terms of "situatedness":

1. Women and men are socially situated beings, who occupy distinct locations in society and history.
2. Social "situatedness" influences philosophical or cognitive activity, including philosophical activity.
3. Almost the whole of philosophy has been written by men.
4. Conclusion: Philosophy is androcentric.

Many of the written discussions that relate to this argument, or to parts of it, do not link it to the question of the androcentricity of philosophy, but make more general claims about knowledge or culture at large. I will examine these discussions here more specifically, in relation only to philosophy and the androcentricity question (although my conclusion has implications for wider contexts).

Many, although not all, of these discussions are influenced by Marxist philosophy. Alison Jaggar, for example, refers to a much-quoted passage from Marx and Engels's *The German Ideology:*

> The class which has the means of the material production at its disposal has control at the same time over the means of the mental production, so that thereby, generally speaking, the ideas of those who lack the means of mental production are subject to it. The ruling ideas are nothing more than the ideal expression of the dominant material relationships, the dominant material relationships grasped as ideas; hence of the relationships which make the one class the ruling one, therefore, the ideas of its dominance.[3]

Jaggar accepts and further explicates this claim:

> I accept Marxist arguments that there is no epistemological standpoint "outside" social reality and that *all* knowledge is

3. *The German Ideology* (New York: International Publishers, 1970), 64; cited in Jaggar, *Feminist Politics and Human Nature,* 359.

shaped by its social origins. In class society, the origins of knowledge are necessarily class origins; there is no standpoint outside all classes. Consequently, in class society, *all* knowledge is bound to represent the standpoint *either* of the rulers *or* the ruled. In this situation, claims that knowledge is objective in the sense of being uninfluenced by class interests are themselves ideological myths. Such claims operate in fact to obscure the ruling-class interests that are promoted by the dominant world view. (*Feminist Politics and Human Nature*, 378; my emphases)

Jaggar adds that "because existing knowledge is grounded on ruling class interests, moreover, it is not a weapon that can simply be taken over by oppressed groups" (378). Her main concern, however, is the relationship between women and men. Hence she broadens Marx's analysis to encompass this relationship by replacing "class" with "gender," claiming that "the concept of women's standpoint presupposes that all knowledge reflects the interests and values of specific social groups" (384).

Similarly, Nancy Hartsock, after quoting the same passage from *The German Ideology,* also argues that

our society . . . is structured not simply by a ruling class dependent on the division of mental from manual labor, but also by a ruling gender, defined by and dependent on the sexual division of labor. Control over the means of mental production belongs to this ruling gender as well as to the ruling class. Thus, one can expect that the categories in which experience is commonly presented are both capitalist and masculine.[4]

But not all written instances of this argument commit themselves to Marxist analysis. Patricia Hill Collins, for example, does not mention Marx at all, writing that "all social thought, including white masculinist and black feminist, reflects the interests and standpoint of its creators. . . . Scholars, publishers, and other experts represent specific interests and credentialing processes, and their knowledge claims must satisfy the epistemological and political criteria of the contexts in which they reside."[5]

4. *Money, Sex and Power,* 9.
5. "Social Construction of Black Feminist Thought," 225. Note that Collins mentions here social thought, not philosophy. Her discussion suggests, however, that she takes "social thought" to include parts of philosophy. I examine Collins's claim as relating to philosophy at large. This does not affect the argument.

In my critique of the first version of this argument I of course accept that philosophy has been written (until the last few decades) almost entirely by men.[6] Nor will I disagree, at least in the present discussion, with the claim that philosophy reflects or is influenced by the values and interests of its authors.[7] I critique here, rather, the third supposition, concerning the difference between men's interests and values and those of women. I do not deny that *some* of men's interests and values differ from *some* of women's interests and values. But I argue that women and men also share many interests and values. And if women and men share interests or values, then those reflected in philosophical theories may be the shared ones, and it is therefore possible that the philosophies are not androcentric. The philosophies *may,* of course, be androcentric; yet their androcentricity cannot be inferred from the type of argument examined here.

There are many interests and values that many women and men share. These include the wish for shelter, nourishment, physical and financial security, and knowledge. I have listed examples of more or less universal interests; however, many nonuniversal ones are also shared by some women and some men. Such include the wish that our company will do better financially in the next quarter, that student enrollment in our university or department will increase, and that the understanding and appreciation of classical music in our society will be fostered. They may also include the wish to save the Amazon rain forest, to promote the practice of yoga in our community, or to fight world illiteracy. Men are not only men (just as women are not only women). They are also workers in our firm, or vegetarians, or our compatriots, or environmentalists, or human beings. And when their interests or values as workers in our firm, as vegetarians, as our compatriots, and so on, are reflected in their writings, the writings need not be androcentric.

Those who hold that men always produce philosophies reflecting interests and values distinct to men may accept that some values and interests are shared with women, but argue that each piece of work and activity reflects *all* the interests and values of its author or agent, and hence that works by men must reflect *also* the nonshared interests and values, and thus must be androcentric. The claim that each work and

---

6. For some important exceptions, see Waithe, *History of Women Philosophers*; McAlister, *Hypatia's Daughters;* Dykeman, *Neglected Canon;* and Warnock, *Women Philosophers.*

7. But I critique a certain understanding of this claim in note 13.

activity reflects *all* the interests and values of its author or agent, however, is implausible, since most of us have many dozens of interests and values. It is unlikely that all of them are reflected in all our works and activities. Furthermore, counterexamples easily come to mind. Consider a man whose inventory of values and interests includes the following: vegetarianism; the promotion of the understanding and appreciation of classical music; winning first prize in the neighborhood's next dahlia-growing competition; being awarded an increase in salary in the next quarter; finding a way to make his baby sleep better at night; and having his daughter do well at school. This, of course, is likely to be only a very partial list of the interests that this man has. Yet even if we consider only these interests, it is difficult to see how watering his dahlias, for example, reflects all the others in the list.

Those who hold that men always produce philosophies reflecting interests and values distinctive to them, and who accept that some interests and values are shared with women, may also argue that those interests and values that influence philosophy (and other endeavors) are exclusively the nonshared ones. However, I see no way of successfully substantiating this claim.

However, those who argue that men always produce philosophies reflecting nonshared interests and values may reject the supposition that there are interests and values shared by women and men. They may argue that such interests are only seemingly shared, since each has, in *all* its aspects that may affect an action or a work, masculine versions and feminine versions. Take, for example, vegetarianism: some of the nutritional supplements that vegetarians need to add to their diets differ for women and for men. And some women are vegetarians because they have feminist-vegetarian beliefs. Similarly, some women who wish to protect the Amazon rain forest may be aware that its disappearance might pose different (in part) environmental health hazards for men and women.

However, for this argument to work it has to be shown that *all* aspects of the interests and values that may affect an action or a work differ for women and for men. But this has not been shown. True, some aspects differ. Yet it is not clear that *they,* rather than the shared aspects, are what affects the action or work in question. For example, a demonstration near a beef factory may be affected by a shared aspect of vegetarianism (such as the view that killing animals for food is wrong), even though some required nutritional supplements differ for women and for men. (Note that some vegetarians may not even know the latter fact, or may know but not care about it.) And although some vegetarians are motivated by feminist-vegetarian rather than by "mainstream" vegetarian views, many, both women and men, are not. Likewise, those interested in protecting the Amazon rain forest *may* be interested in the issue for reasons that have nothing to do with differences between women and men, and their actions and works to preserve it may be affected by shared aspects of the concern.

It might be answered that all that I have shown here is that *some* aspects of the interests and values may be shared, and some may not, and that this is insufficient to support my critique. However, while the argument I examine here has to hold that no aspects of all values and interests of all women and men are shared, I do not have to show that they are all shared. It is sufficient to show that it is very likely that some are. Since if it is plausible that women and men share some values and interests (or some relevant aspects thereof), then those that affect or are reflected in philosophy may be the shared ones. They may also, of course, be those that are not shared. However, to know which is the case we have to check, again, each instance individually, much as we had to do in Chapter 2. My claim is more moderate, and hence also easier to defend, than the claim I critique.

Another version of the claim, influenced by a certain interpretation of Marx, may suggest that no values or interests that influence knowledge are shared by women and men. According to Jaggar, "in class society, *all* knowledge is bound to represent the standpoint *either* of the rulers *or* the ruled" (*Feminist Politics and Human Nature,* 378; my emphases). In her version of this claim, the rulers and the ruled who have no interest in common are, of course, men and women. However, no evidence is suggested for this either/or claim. Moreover, those Jaggar regards as the "real" rulers and "real" ruled, who have no interests in common, are distinguished by gender. For Marx, however, the "real" rulers and ruled are members of different socio-economic strata, and it is *they* who share no interests,[8] whereas women and men of the same socio-economic stratum do share many interests. A third theorist might assert this claim with regard to other groups, such as our nation and others, or old and young, with a similar lack of substantiation. Thus, this version of the argument too is not helpful in demonstrating the androcentricity of philosophy.

Another version of this argument might rest on certain interpretations

8. There may be different interpretations of Marx on this point, some suggesting that he believed that members of different social-economic strata may share some interests, but I follow Jaggar's interpretation here.

of Nietzsche or Foucault, according to which *everything* we do, including our intellectual and scholarly work, is a means of achieving domination over others.[9] It might be suggested that values, activities, and works that do not appear to be means of domination are merely more subtle, sophisticated, and therefore more effective means of domination, since "power is tolerable only on condition that it masks a substantial part of itself. Its success is proportional to its ability to hide its own mechanisms."[10] In such a view, people's real interests are not in furthering vegetarianism, the appreciation of classical music, and so on but, rather, in achieving greater hegemony over others. This is what genuinely initiates and directs people's activities, and all other values and interests are actually the masked means for achieving domination.[11] If this is the case, it might be argued, men's real interest is to dominate women, and this is what truly motivates and directs all of men's works and activities, including, of course, their philosophical ones.

Let us assume, for the sake of discussion, that the true interest of all people is, indeed, the domination of others.[12] Who are these "others" that one has an interest in dominating? They could be almost anyone: people of another race or nation; members of another socio-economic stratum; supporters of another political party; economic competitors; colleagues in one's department; the next-door neighbor; environmentalists or anti-environmentalists; and of course, people of the other gender. Women and men who belong to the same group (for example, vegetarians, members of a certain financial firm) may well have the same, shared interest in dominating members of another group (for example, nonvegetarians or members of another firm). This is because, as noted earlier, men are not only men; they are also vegetarians or nonvegetarians, environmentalists, music lovers, property owners, or our compatriots.

---

9. Such interpretations could refer to passages such as "Knowledge works as a tool of power" or "power and knowledge directly imply one another; . . . there is no power relation without the correlative constitution of a field of knowledge, nor any knowledge that does not presuppose and constitute at the same time power relations." Friedrich Nietzsche, *The Will to Power*, trans. Walter Kaufmann and R. J. Hollingdale (London: Weidenfeld and Nicolson, 1968), sec. 480; Foucault, *Discipline and Punish*, 27.

10. Foucault, *History of Sexuality, Vol. 1*, 86.

11. The term "domination" is difficult to define. In the following discussion, it will be used interchangeably with "control," "hegemony," and "oppression of others." Under the term's common usage, one dominates others when what are understood to be one's interests are illegitimately satisfied at the expense of what are understood to be the interests of others. Domination is also related to the ability to inflict social, psychological, or physical sanctions upon others.

12. But the claim is critiqued in note 13.

The problems noted earlier are pertinent also regarding the other two versions of this argument. Take, for example, the second version, which instead of emphasizing that philosophies are authored by men, takes them to be influenced by the culture, civilization, or social reality in which they were written. In this version, Western philosophy is claimed to be androcentric, since an androcentric culture, or social reality, is bound to give rise to androcentric products. However, although Western culture does encompass an androcentric component, it incorporates many other elements also. Among these are included, as noted earlier, the interest in nourishment, personal and financial security, health, the aspiration to save the Amazon rain forest, and the interest in knowing the truth. The products of a culture *may,* of course, reflect its androcentric element, but may express other components of the culture as well.

Again, it may be argued that *all* the elements or interests of a culture are reflected in *each* of its products, and hence the androcentric elements of Western culture must be reflected in all Western philosophies. However, the notion that *all* the many elements of a culture are reflected in *each and every one* of its products is, again, implausible, for reasons similar to those already suggested earlier: every culture includes a plethora of values and interests. It is very unlikely that *all* of them are reflected in each work and activity of that culture. One might also maintain that all values in a culture have masculine and feminine versions. There is a masculine version of shelter, health, personal and financial security, classical music, protecting the Amazon rain forest, and the interest in knowing the truth, as well as a feminine version of these values. However, the critique of this conception suggested earlier applies here as well. One might argue, moreover, that although there are many components to our culture, or social environment, for some reason the androcentric ones are those reflected in the philosophical works. However, as I have noted, it is unclear how this claim could be successfully substantiated. Similar difficulties would inhere in arguments of this type based on women's and men's different "situatedness."

The argument suggesting that X's book, on any philosophical subject, must be androcentric since X is a man is as strong as the argument suggesting that X's book, on any philosophical subject (or any subject in any field), must be anti-Muslim since X is a Hindu living in India, or that X's book, on any subject, must include pro-vegetarian themes since X is a vegetarian, or that X's book, on any subject, must include messages calling for the appreciation of classical music since X is a great fan of classical music. Interestingly, the argument from distinct values and interests is rarely or never accepted when applied to groups other than women and men. We do not suppose that *all* the activities and works of people who are, say, Christians, environmentalists, or nationalist Croats or Serbs reflect their particular interests or the distinct components of their identities as Christians, environmentalists, Croats or Serbs, even when they are devout Christians or enthusiastic environmentalists, and so on. It is surprising, then, that this argument is accepted when applied to men and women.

This discussion is not intended, however, to assert that there is no, or cannot be any, androcentricity in philosophy, or that the nonshared or androcentric interests and values of authors, or the androcentric elements in culture, can never influence or be reflected in philosophies. It only suggests that androcentric elements in culture and nonshared values and interests do not *necessarily* influence philosophies. It is *possible* for a certain component of the social reality, or culture, or personality, to influence philosophical works, and thus it is also possible for an androcentric component to influence a work and make it androcentric. However, to know whether a philosophical work is, in fact, androcentric, other arguments for the androcentricity of philosophy, discussed in the other chapters of this book, must be examined. The argument examined in the present chapter is insufficient for this purpose. A weaker form of this argument can make us more alert to the possibility that philosophy is androcentric; since we know that philosophy has been written predominantly by men, and that androcentric elements do exist in many parts of Western culture, we should be sensitive to the possibility that philosophy may be androcentric, and be inclined to inquire whether this is the case. However, this sensitivity or inclination cannot come in lieu of the examination itself.[13]

13. The discussion hitherto granted that philosophy always reflects or is influenced by the values and interests of its authors, and that *everything* we do, including our intellectual and scholarly work, is a means of achieving domination over others. As I tried to show, the argument for the androcentricity of philosophy discussed in this chapter is insufficient to show that philosophy is androcentric even if these two presuppositions are accepted. However, I should also like to explain here why I believe that they should not be accepted.

As for the first supposition, much depends on how one understands the claim "philosophy always reflects or is influenced by the values and interests of its authors." If it is taken to mean (as it frequently is) that philosophy always reflects or is influenced by the *vested* interests and values of its authors, I think it is incorrect. If it is taken to mean that philosophy can also reflect or be influenced by the values of good, professional research that is as neutral as possible, I agree. Since these are the values and interests that many philosophers and researchers indeed entertain, it is only reasonable to expect that they will sometimes influence research. Since we are not influenced by all our values and interests at all times and occasions, it is possible for a philosophical research to be influenced only by vested values and interests; to be influenced by vested values and interests as well as by the value of good, professional research that is as neutral as possible; and to be influenced only by the value of good, professional research that is as neutral as possible. It may be objected here that the vested interests are somehow always present, or that they always inform research, but the considerations suggested above concerning shared and nonshared interests apply similarly here. We cannot be certain that our research is not influenced by vested interests; nor, however, can we be sure that it is. The generalization that our research *must* be influenced by vested interests is incorrect.

Interestingly, notwithstanding the prevalence of this generalization, I have found no good proof for it. Frequently, it is simply presented as a dogma. On other occasions it is supported by some examples where research that seemed uninfluenced by vested interests is shown to be influenced by them. But this is a problematic extrapolation from some cases—interesting as they are—to all. Perhaps we can never be sure that we completely succeed in overcoming the lure of our vested interests, only try as hard as we can to do so, and reach, through various techniques, higher degrees of probability that we have succeeded in these efforts. But the supposition that we in principle *cannot* but be influenced by our vested interests is incorrect. Helpful discussions of this issue can be found in Susan Haack's *Defending Science—Within Reason, Manifesto of a Passionate Moderate*, and *Evidence and Inquiry.*

For the sake of discussion, I have also granted that what all people are really interested in is dominating others and that this interest lurks behind and influences everything they do. But again, more frequently than not, no effort is made to prove this sweeping generalization, and it is simply presented as dogma. When proof for the generalization is offered, it consists, again, of examples in which the interest in domination does play a part, followed by an explicit or implicit argument by induction generalizing from a few cases to all, while ignoring many counterexamples. Alternatives—such as that what really lies behind and influences everything we do is actually our will to be loved by others, or find meaning, or destroy ourselves, or know the truth—are no less plausible.

This discussion on shared and unshared interests and values is also relevant for some work on standpoint epistemology. Some discussions seem to suppose that if two groups (say, women and men; or white feminists and black feminists) have distinct social positions, identities, or cultures, they must also have distinct interests and values, which must also produce distinct philosophies, epistemologies, and views. But while women and men, or white feminists and black feminists (or Hispanic feminists, lesbian feminists, and so on) have some unshared interests and values, they also have many shared ones, and it may be that on many points the shared, rather than unshared, interests and values influence these groups' philosophies and works.

7

Philosophies and Mentalities

I

Probably the most commonly found type of argument for the androcentricity of philosophy is based on claims that find parallels between philosophy and men's, rather than women's, minds, mentalities, or psyches.[1] These parallels are argued to show that the character of philosophy suits, or reflects, the mentalities of men rather than of women. Nel Noddings and Nancy Tuana, for example, rely in such arguments on Carol Gilligan's claims concerning men's tendency toward "justice morality" and women's tendency toward "care morality."[2] "Justice morality" is more procedural, universal, objective, abstract, precise, dualistic, individualist, rule-oriented, disputative, nonemotional, and noncontextual. "Care morality" is more intuitive and emotional, contextual, empathetic, relational, personal, concrete, and less oriented toward procedures, generalizations, objectivity, certainty, or precision. But moral philosophy is claimed to have the characteristics of justice morality. As such, it agrees with men's mentalities rather than with women's.

Likewise, Merrill B. Hintikka and Jaakko Hintikka argue that "women are generally more sensitive to, and likely to assign more importance to, relational characteristics (e.g., interdependencies) than males, and less likely to think in terms of independent discrete units. Conversely,

1. Although the terms "minds," "mentalities," "psyches," "emotional tendencies," and so on, differ in meaning and application, I use them interchangeably in the discussion ahead.
2. Noddings, *Caring;* Tuana, *Woman and the History of Philosophy,* 118–19; Gilligan, *In a Different Voice.*

males generally prefer what is separable and manipulatable."[3] But "it is arguable that Western philosophical thought has been overemphasizing such ontological models as postulate a given fixed supply of discrete individuals, individuated by their intrinsic or essential (non-relational) properties" (146). Similarly, Nancy C. M. Hartsock argues that "different psychic experiences both structure and are reinforced by the differing patterns of men's and women's activity required by the sexual divisions of labor, and are thereby replicated as epistemology and ontology."[4] Men's minds or mentalities are characterized by dualism, abstractness, and a hostile and combative attitude, whereas "women's construction of self in relation to others leads . . . toward opposition to dualisms of any sort; valuation of concrete, everyday life; a sense of a variety of connectednesses and continuities both with other persons and with the natural world" (242). It is thus no coincidence for her that, when women political theorists write about power, they stress qualities such as energy and capacity.

The arguments can be presented in the following form:

1. The characteristics of men's minds or mentalities differ from those of women's.
2. The characteristics of philosophy parallel, or suit, the characteristics of men's minds or mentalities rather than those of women's minds or mentalities.
3. Conclusion: Philosophy is androcentric.

In what follows I will argue that arguments of this type are problematic in their representation of women's and men's mentalities, their representation of philosophy, and their representation of the correspondence of philosophy to men's rather than to women's mentalities.

2

In this section I suggest that women's and men's minds are in many ways similar, and that when they differ, the dissimilarities are too slight to sustain the argument for the androcentricity of philosophy. When average differences between women's and men's minds are found, they are

---

3. "How Can Language Be Sexist?" 146.
4. *Money, Sex and Power*, 240.

very small. Moreover, within-gender variability is larger than between-gender variability. Put differently, the average differences between women's and men's minds are significantly smaller than the differences that exist *among* women or *among* men.

Consider the populations of two imaginary countries, A and B. The populations are similar in that in both, about half the population engages in sports. Suppose that we also find that the population in A engages in sports, on average, slightly more than does the population in B (the difference, however, is small). Moreover, suppose that we found that there is a wide variability among the inhabitants of A, as there is among the inhabitants of B: while some inhabitants of A exercise several hours a day, many others in A do not exercise at all. The same is true for the inhabitants of B. (The small average difference may be also influenced by the habit of a small minority of inhabitants of A, say, three percent, to exercise all day long, while only a quarter of a percent of the inhabitants of B do so.) Being an inhabitant of A or an inhabitant of B, then, is a poor predictor of degree of engagement in sports. Furthermore, suppose that the inclination to engage in sports is found to depend heavily, in the populations of both countries, on one's socio-economic class and level of education. I believe that in such circumstances it would be wrong to typify A as the "sporting nation" and B as the "slack nation" (or "nonphysical" nation), or to present, on this basis, exercising as an "A activity" and, say, resting as a "B activity." The same would be true, I suggest, concerning differences between women's and men's minds (in those cases where differences are found at all).

The question of the difference between women's and men's mentalities should be determined by empirical evidence. Some arguments, however, do not present empirical research in sufficient detail. Hartsock points to biological and psychodynamic theories when she discusses the differences between women's and men's mentalities. But such theories are *explanations* for the supposed differences, not *proofs* or *evidence* that the supposed differences exist. They cannot be relied on as testimony that there are indeed such differences. For that purpose, empirical evidence has to be sought. Hintikka and Hintikka do present some such evidence, but very limited in extent. Gilligan presents a much wider body of empirical evidence, which I discuss ahead. I argue here that empirical evidence suggests that women's and men's minds do not differ significantly.

Eleanor Emmons Maccoby and Carol Nagy Jacklin's complex and careful study *The Psychology of Sex Differences* can serve as a good starting point for this discussion. From their comprehensive and critical review of works on sex differences they conclude that "the two sexes are equally interested in social . . . stimuli and are equally proficient at learning through imitation of models" (349). Likewise, girls are not more dependent on caretakers, do not spend more time interacting with playmates, are not better at understanding others' emotional reactions, and are not more reluctant to remain alone (ibid.). Boys and girls are equally susceptible to persuasive communication, and boys "appear to be more likely to accept peer-group values when they conflict with their own" (350). There are no differences in self-confidence and self-esteem, proficiency in cognitive processing and inhibition of previously learned responses, analytic abilities, and achievement motivation (350–51). Findings were ambiguous, or there was too little evidence for conclusions about differences in activity levels, competitiveness, dominance, compliance, passivity, tendency toward fear, timidity and anxiety, and nurturance and "maternal" behavior (352–54). Maccoby and Jacklin did find, however, that boys on average have a lower verbal ability and a higher visual-spatial and mathematical ability than girls, and that boys are more aggressive than girls (351–52). However, the differences between boys and girls in the first three categories are small. For verbal and visual skills, for example, the differences are five percent. As Anne Fausto-Sterling explains, this means that "if one looks at the variation (from lowest to highest performance) of spatial ability in a mixed population of males and females, 5 percent of it at most can be accounted for on the basis of sex. The other 95 percent of the variation is due to individual differences that have nothing to do with being male or female."[5] For aggression, differences were more considerable. However, later studies show that the males indeed score higher for aggression that produces pain or physical injury or in overt aggression (for example, hitting, pushing, or threatening to do so), but that differences are very small, or girls score higher, for aggression that produces psychological or social harm, or in relational aggression (for example, excluding from group, ostracizing, withdrawing friendship or threatening to do so).[6] If philosophy is taken to be an aggressive activity, the aggression seems to be of the latter type, where differences are nonexistent or small. These findings should also make us wary of inferring from one category to another: differences in physical aggression do not attest to differences in verbal or indirect aggression;

---

5. *Myths of Gender*, 33.
6. Crick and Grotepeter, "Relational Aggression"; Eagly and Steffen, "Gender and Aggressive Behavior."

likewise, differences in aggression do not attest to differences in self-confidence, competitiveness, dominance, or susceptibility to persuasive communication. We cannot deduce from the existence of differences in one category the existence of differences in another.

Jacklin also reviews the ten most common methodological mistakes made by researchers on sex-related differences.[7] She notes that there is a "bias toward publishing . . . citing and reprinting positive findings. If a positive instance is found, it is much easier to publish . . . [and] it becomes a part of the literature. . . . If one could easily publish findings of similarities and if they were abstracted and indexed, these non-differences would also become the material for summaries of sex related differences" (267–68). Another important problem is that "white, upper-middle-class, educated, largely Anglo-Saxon populations are disproportionately used, while generalizations are erroneously made to all." The most pervasive problem in such studies, however, is "the number of variables that are confounded with sex" (271).

Many of these difficulties have remained prevalent in the research on sex differences. Carol Gilligan has argued that girls and women tend toward a care mentality, and boys and men toward a justice mentality (although, as Michele Moody-Adams and Joan C. Williams note, Gilligan is not completely clear on this thesis).[8] Her conclusions are based on boys' and girls' replies to moral dilemmas she presented to them (such as the Heinz dilemma: Heinz's wife will die without a medicine they cannot afford; what should Heinz do?), men's and women's descriptions of certain pictures, and interviews with women who had to face decisions on abortion. However, the evidence Gilligan presents for her conclusions is

---

7. See her "Methodological Issues."

8. Moody-Adams, "Gender," 197–98; Williams, "Deconstructing Gender," 813. Some of Gilligan's claims suggest that she wishes to discuss the differences between care and justice moralities, not to make a point about women and men. Thus, she claims that "the different voice . . . is characterized *not by gender but theme.* Its association with women is an empirical observation, and it is primarily through women's voices that I trace its development. But this association is not absolute, and the contrasts between male and female voices are presented here to highlight a distinction between two modes of thought and to focus a problem of interpretation rather than to represent a generalization about either sex." *In a Different Voice,* 2; my emphasis. However, Gilligan also argues that her book aims to provide psychologists with tools for understanding *women's* development, as well as to give "a clearer representation of *women's* development" (3; my emphasis). She subtitles her book "Psychological Theory and Women's Development," and writes that "in the different voice of *women* lies the truth of an ethic of care" (173; my emphasis). Notwithstanding this ambivalence, Gilligan will be read here—as she commonly is—as claiming that the mentalities or minds of women and men differ.

problematic. As Moody-Adams notes, the abortion study does not rely on a representative sample (even in Gilligan's own opinion), and it is not clear that if the women of that sample had been asked about rape, sexual harassment, or discrimination in the workplace, rather than about abortion, they still would have used the categories of care.[9] Other difficulties exemplify the problems Jacklin mentions: Gilligan's research, too, seems not to have taken into account women and men over forty, and apparently concentrates on urban, North American, white Anglo-Saxon middle-class or upper-middle-class populations. Moreover, Gilligan's study, as well as the many empirical undertakings confirming her findings, repeat what Jacklin calls the most pervasive problem of such research: no strict controls are used on variables such as occupation or education (or age, marital status, extent of joint household decision-making, and sex of the protagonist described in the dilemma). As Jyotsna Vasudev points out in her discussion of a work by Gilligan and Jane Attanucci, in studies where strict controls were employed, no consequential differences were found between women and men.[10] This implies that the determining factors for having care or justice mentalities are, in fact, not masculinity or femininity, but education, economic class, and so on. In their reply to Vasudev, Gilligan and Attanucci seem to accept Vasudev's claim that the determining factors for favoring justice or care are education, economic class, and so on, yet claim that gender categories are still meaningful, since women tend to earn less than men. Thus, they point out that "Vasudev (1988) argues from a justice standpoint that . . . when psychologists control for socioeconomic status, sex differences disappear. Yet women

9. "Gender," 202–4, 208.

10. "Sex Differences," 241. Vasudev is referring to Gilligan and Attanucci, "Two Moral Orientations." Vasudev cites, among others, Lawrence J. Walker's literature review in "Sex Differences in the Development of Moral Reasoning: A Critical Review," *Child Development* 55 (1984): 677–91, and his "Experiential and Cognitive Sources of Moral Development in Adulthood," *Human Development* 29 (1986): 113–24; as well as Jyotsna Vasudev and Raymond C. Hummel, "Moral Stage Sequence and Principled Reasoning in an Indian Sample," *Human Development* 30 (1987): 105–18. For a response to Walker, see Diana Baumrind, "Sex Differences in Moral Reasoning: Response to Walker's (1984) Conclusion That There Are None," *Child Development* 57 (1986): 511–21. For Walker's reply, see "Sex Differences in the Development of Moral Reasoning: A Rejoinder to Baumrind," *Child Development* 57 (1986): 522–26. In other studies, moral orientation seemed to be related to age rather than sex. See Michael W. Pratt, Gail Golding, William Hunter, and Joan Norris, "From Inquiry to Judgment: Age and Sex Differences in Patterns of Adult Moral Thinking and Information-Seeking," *International Journal of Ageing and Human Development* 27 (1988): 109–24.

and men are not socioeconomic equals."[11] Moreover, "our disagreement with Vasudev stems from the fact that we observe women and men to stand in different positions within American society and within Western culture and to engage in different activities, which we consider morally germane" (455).

Nevertheless, if the determining factors for the use of care and justice mentalities are economic class and other such factors, then justice and care mentalities should be seen as primarily those of people of the relevant economic classes. Care mentality would be women's in merely a derivative, secondary way, and only because women (unfortunately) have a higher representation than men in the lower socio-economic strata, which are typified by care mentality in a more direct way. Moreover, other groups that are overrepresented in the lower socio-economic strata have a "claim" to care mentality no less than do women. And if these other groups have an even higher representation than women in lower socio-economic strata, they have an even stronger "claim" to care mentality. It should also be acknowledged that care mentality is not the mentality of all women, but only of those who belong to lower socio-economic strata; and if women's overrepresentation in lower economic strata decreases (as is hoped), the higher prevalence of care ethics among women will decrease as well. Noting factors that are of more direct relevance to the researched phenomena is common in social or psychological research. For example, Bonnie Yegidis Lewis discusses Straus, Gelles, and Steinmetz's claim that "black males showed the highest levels of spouse abuse."[12] Lewis's empirical research found "no difference between the two groups by race of either the respondents or their male partners, when the variable social status was controlled. Thus, when the target population is of lower socio-economic status, there is no reason to suspect that blacks are more likely to display wife abuse than whites" (9). Although, of course, it is clear that Gilligan and Attanucci would not argue in this fashion in the present case, if to follow the logic of their reply to Vasudev,

11. "Much Ado About . . . Knowing?" 451 (abstract). The intent of Gilligan and Attanucci's remark that "Vasudev argues from a justice standpoint" is not clear. It may mean that women or feminists need not heed controlled empirical research, or that it and the uncontrolled empirical research of the sort Gilligan presents in her book are equally reliable. But such interpretations of Gilligan and Attanucci's remark would present them as holding highly unfeasible views.

12. Lewis, "Psychological Factors," 1–10; M. Straus, R. J. Gelles, and S. Steinmetz, *Behind Closed Doors: Violence in the American Family* (New York: Doubleday, 1980), cited in Lewis.

Lewis would be answered that we should still talk of wife abuse as a "black behavior" since blacks and whites "are not socioeconomic equals" and "stand in different positions within American society . . . and . . . engage in different activities."

In their reply to Vasudev, Gilligan and Attanucci also cite some evidence concerning sex differences. They point out, for example, the "striking sex differences in such morally relevant behavior as the incidence of violent crime, or . . . the sex differences in the composition of the prison population" ("Much Ado About . . . Knowing?" 451). I believe, however, that these facts do not strengthen Gilligan's claims about justice orientation and care orientation, since participation in violent crimes is in conflict with justice ethics no less than with care ethics. A man who robs a bank or murders a passer-by shows, of course, no empathy, but also no concern for rules or justice. In fact, many, and perhaps most, violent crimes exhibit characteristics associated with care mentality more than those associated with justice mentality; many of them seem to be performed in an emotional state which emphasizes the immediate, concrete, and nonuniversalized.[13]

Gilligan and Attanucci also point out that common experience supports the view that there are differences between women's and men's mentalities:

> A friendly colleague said to us recently: "But everyone knows there are sex differences." Why then such controversy, we thought. . . . Yet the discussion of sex differences and moral development within the field of psychology often seems premised on the assumption that common knowledge about sex differences is misleading. . . .
>
> Thus Vasudev (1988), commenting on our recent paper (Gilligan & Attanucci, 1988), makes what she terms the "justified demand" that we join our "good ideas" with "strong" rather than "weak data," so that our ideas will not be dismissed by others as "trivial." (451)

However, Vasudev does not seem to presuppose that common experience is misleading, only that it is insufficient and—being frequently influenced by stereotypes and crude generalizations—should not be relied upon. It

---

13. For further difficulties in the "prison population argument," see Moody-Adams, "Gender," 198–200.

should be remembered that common experience also led many to believe for a long time that wife battering, sexual harassment, and rape are quite infrequent phenomena, while research has shown that they are more common than was popularly believed. Common experience, then, does not seem sufficiently reliable. If Gilligan's and others' research is questionable because it does not use strict controls, then common experience is even more so.

Gilligan and Attanucci also note that their research dealt only with the educationally advantaged (452). Thus, one factor is controlled in their study. However, they do not use other controls, nor do they write how strictly they employed this one.

Subsequent research repeats and confirms that differences between women and men, when such exist, are small; that the differences among men, and the differences among women, are larger than the differences between men and women; that non-sex-related factors determine people's intellectual and emotional characteristics far more than do sex-related factors; and that sex is an unhelpful predictor of mental abilities. Alice Stuhlmacher and Amy Walters conclude their discussion of women's and men's negotiating abilities by writing that "although the men in our analysis appeared to negotiate more favorable settlements for themselves than the women, the gap appears very narrow indeed."[14] Janet Shibley Hyde found that although females are less aggressive than males, "within-gender variability is larger than the variability between genders."[15] In another study, Sara Jaffee and Hyde examined one hundred and thirteen studies of moral reasoning and argue that "the results of this meta-analysis do not indicate that the care and justice orientations are strongly gender differentiated. Moreover, the results of the moderator analysis support previous findings that the type of moral reasoning an individual uses is highly sensitive to the context and content of the dilemma."[16] Furthermore, "the finding that 73% of the studies that measured care reasoning and 72% of the studies that measured justice reasoning failed to find significant gender differences, leads us to conclude that, although distinct moral orientations may exist, these orientations are not strongly associated with gender" (719).

But if both women and men show a combination of "male" and "female" characteristics, if the average differences between men and women

14. "Gender Differences in Negotiating Outcome," 674.
15. "How Large Are Gender Differences in Aggression?" 731.
16. "Gender Differences in Moral Orientation," 721.

are slight, if being a man or a woman is such a poor predictor of one's mental abilities, if women's and men's qualities are influenced by so many non-gender-related factors, and if men differ among themselves radically, and women differ among themselves radically (and more so than men as a group differ from women as a group), then the argument that philosophy is androcentric since it parallels or suits men's mentalities more than women's does not hold.

3

Suppose, however, that contrary to what has just been argued, substantial differences (in characteristics that are relevant to philosophical activity) between women's and men's mentalities are found, and between-gender differences are significantly larger than within-gender differences. Assume that, say, beliefs, stereotypes, education, and other forms of acculturation succeed in significantly changing not only women's and men's *perceptions* of their mentalities, but also their mentalities themselves. Some such beliefs, stereotypes, and so on, could operate as self-fulfilling prophecies, bringing into reality what they have described. Or suppose that we should accept Gilligan and Attanucci's view and refrain from distinguishing between variables such as education, socio-economic status, and so on, on the one hand, and the way women and men are, on the other hand. Since women are overrepresented among the poor, for example, certain characteristics more prevalent among the poor will be seen as women's.

I believe that the argument for the androcentricity of philosophy examined in this chapter would still be problematic, since we may believe that the overrepresentation of women in certain groups, or the effect of a certain education, acculturation, or self-fulfilling prophecies on women (or any other group) may not be good, and we may choose to reject it. As Susan Haack has argued, there may be cases where we think a philosophy not suitable to a certain education or life experience, but still choose to change the education or life experience rather than reject the philosophy.[17] Take the following example: there was a time when, because of their nurture and acculturation, women neither voted nor, for the most part, felt competent to do so. But this did not mean that participation in the democratic process did not agree with women, or that they should

17. "Science 'From a Feminist Perspective,'" 17.

have had their own way of exerting political influence, more appropriate to their nurture and experiences. Rather, it was thought that women's nurture and acculturation should change to suit participation in the democratic process. The *value* of the property believed to be more characteristic of women than of men, then, has to be taken into account. If women (or men) are acculturated to have a certain trait that is not a virtue, we should try to change that acculturation. (The argument here, then, is somewhat similar to that presented in Chapter 3, where it was claimed that, in some cases, we should strive to change or reject, rather than yield to, stereotypes, social practices, and associations.) As a general rule, we should discuss the *value* of a trait, not only its prevalence, in order to decide whether it should be continued and developed. This is true, of course, also of other cases. Thus, for example, if we believe smoking to be harmful, we would recommend quitting even to those who are accustomed to it. And if some people, even if they belong to a certain group (for example, Westerners), are not accustomed to a certain diet, exercise, or meditation, we may still recommend these practices if we think they are beneficial. The fact that Westerners are not accustomed to them is no reason for their rejection.

The prevalence of a certain way of thinking or behaving, then, is not a sufficient reason for accepting it. And if some people, or groups of people, are not used to certain ways of thinking or behaving, it is not clear that these ways of thinking or behaving should change, rather than peoples' habits. Thus, if women's and men's mentalities are indeed sufficiently different (which I doubt), and if women's mentalities are commendable, then men should try to change their habits and outlook and adopt women's. Likewise, if men's mentalities are worthy, women too should be able to enjoy them. And it may be that both women and men should alter some aspects of their mentalities. The conservative claim, that "this is what should be done since this is the way we have always done it" is unsatisfactory.

Hence, even if it were satisfactorily shown that, because of education, acculturation, popular beliefs, or overrepresentation in certain groups, women's mentalities do not suit philosophy (or a certain philosophy), this would not in itself suffice for deducing that philosophy should be rejected or replaced by an alternative. As noted in Chapter 1, the term "androcentric" should be understood not only descriptively as what "suits men's experiences or minds more than women's, or involves male discrimination against women, or leads to the domination of women by men," but also normatively, as what *"should be rejected, or reformed,* because it suits men's experiences or minds more than women's, or involves male discrimination against women, or leads to the domination of women by men." Even if it were the case, then, that philosophy temporarily suits men's experiences or minds more than women's, this in itself is still insufficient to show that the philosophy is androcentric, since it may be that women's experiences and minds, rather than philosophy, should change.

Assume that it were somehow shown that biological, rather than social, factors are responsible for various differences that are claimed to exist between women and men. Would this suggest that these differences should be maintained? The answer, again, is negative. As already argued by Janet Radcliffe Richards, following "biology" or "nature" is not the only consideration we take into account when deciding between alternatives, nor is it the overriding one.[18] Some of us may agree, for example, that being unfaithful to one's spouse is more natural than being faithful to her or him, but we may still advocate fidelity because we see it as mandatory for meaningful and worthy relationships. Likewise, resolving conflicts by physical violence may be seen as more natural or "biological" than settling them by discussion or negotiation, but the latter alternatives may still be deemed preferable. Or we may think that keeping promises and observing agreements is not natural, but still advisable. Thus, even if it were shown that a certain way of thinking is unnatural to one of the sexes, it could still be claimed that if that way of thinking is better than others, it should be adopted even by those to whom it does not come naturally.

4

I believe that the arguments critiqued in this chapter are also problematic in another way. However, this problem arises only for those who support feminism and oppose male chauvinism. As already has been argued in different ways and from diverse perspectives by Susan Haack, Alan Soble, and Jean Grimshaw, the belief that women and men have different minds and mentalities is shared by the scholars discussed in this chapter, on the one hand, and male chauvinists, on the other.[19] Their characterizations of women and men are also frequently analogous, as are the types of arguments they use to demonstrate their views. Of course, this in itself

18. See Richards, *Sceptical Feminist*, 71–72.
19. Haack, "Best Man," 175; Soble, "Feminist Epistemology and Women Scientists"; Grimshaw, *Philosophy and Feminist Thinking*, 258.

does not show that the belief in differences between women's and men's mentalities is unsubstantiated (other sections in this chapter aim to show that). Yet those who support feminism and oppose male chauvinism should observe the similarities in methods of argumentation and in many conclusions, and need to clarify, to avoid inconsistency, why they support one view but not the other. Many of Schopenhauer's portrayals of women's morality, for example, are not very different from Gilligan's or Hartsock's:

> Women . . . always see only what is nearest to them, cling to the present. . . . In consequence of her weaker faculty of reason, woman shares less in the advantages and disadvantages that this entails. . . . Since her intuitive understanding sees quite clearly what is near, but has a narrow range of vision into which the distant object does not enter. . . .
>
> . . . they are inferior to men in the matter of justice, honesty, and conscientiousness. For in consequence of their weak faculty of reason, that which is present, intuitively perceptual, immediately real, exercise over them a power against which abstract thoughts, established maxims, fixed resolves, and generally a consideration of the past and future, the absent and distant, are seldom able to do much.[20]

Similarly, Otto Weininger claims that

> a woman cannot grasp that one must act from principle; as she has no continuity she does not experience the necessity for logical support of her mental processes. Hence the ease with which women assume opinions. . . . Woman resents any attempt to require from her that her thoughts should be logical.[21]

Many of the implications of the arguments examined here are also similar to those of the arguments of male chauvinists: if women's and

20. Arthur Schopenhauer, "On Women," in *Parerga and Paralipomena: Short Philosophical Essays,* trans. E.F.J. Payne (Oxford: Clarendon Press, 1974), 2:616, 617. The analogy, of course, is not complete, since some of Schopenhauer's descriptions of women are not matched by the feminist authors I have mentioned.

21. Otto Weininger, *Sex and Character,* translator not named (New York: Putnam, n.d.), 149. For more examples of male chauvinist characterizations of women that accord with this type of feminist thinking, see, for example, Georg Simmel, "The Relative and the Absolute in the Problem of the Sexes," in his *On Women, Sexuality and Love,* trans. Guy Oakes (New Haven: Yale University Press, 1984), 112.

men's minds are as different as male chauvinists and the scholars mentioned above claim them to be, then many occupations indeed do not suit women. If we follow this line of reasoning, women's underrepresentation and lower income in these occupations may be justified. Nor would it be clear that if discrimination exists, it should be fought against; eliminating educational, psychological, and social discrimination, or entering into (what are taken to be) male professions may change (what are taken to be) women's mentalities, which some of the scholars mentioned above wish to preserve and develop. Some writers call both for developing women's supposedly specifically "female" mentalities and for women's equal participation in what they take to be a man's world. However, as argued by Jyotsna Vasudev, concerning some occupations (namely, some scientific, technological, legal, and economic functions), the two visions are in conflict, unless one deems it viable that these spheres will change to the radical extent necessary to suit what are taken to be the distinct characteristics of women's minds.[22] It is frequently said in such cases that the difference lies in the attitude toward "women's characteristics." While male chauvinists despise them, feminists such as those mentioned above respect them and prefer them to "men's characteristics." However, many chauvinists, too, respect "women's characteristics," praising or even admiring them.

Similarly, feminist biological arguments are akin to, and as lax as, male chauvinist biological arguments. For example, according to Hartsock's somewhat Manichaean[23] account of women and men, "in a literal sense, the sperm . . . is cut off from its source and lost. Perhaps we should not wonder, then, at the masculinist preoccupation with death, and the feeling that growth is 'impersonal,' not of fundamental concern to oneself."[24] On the other hand, women's

> construction of self in relation to others leads in an opposite direction—toward opposition to dualisms of any sort. . . . Women experience others and themselves along a continuum whose dimensions are evidenced in Adrienne Rich's argument that the child carried for nine months can be defined "*neither* as me or as not-me." . . . Finally, the unity of mental and manual labor

22. See Vasudev, "Sex Differences," 240.

23. I borrow this term from Elshtain, "New Feminist Scholarship," 12–16, although I use it slightly differently.

24. *Money, Sex and Power*, 244. Hartsock mentions her debt in this discussion to Bataille's *Death and Sexuality*.

and the directly sensuous nature of much of women's work leads
to a more profound unity . . . than is experienced by the male
worker in capitalism. The unity grows from the fact that wom-
en's bodies, unlike men's, can be themselves instruments of production: in pregnancy, giving birth, or lactation. (242–43;
Hartsock's emphasis. See also 237, 257)[25]

This is as convincing as Schopenhauer's claim that "as the weaker, they
[women] are by nature dependent not on force but cunning; hence their
instinctive artfulness and ineradicable tendency to tell lies" ("On
Women," 617).

5

In the argument suggesting that there are parallels between philosophy
and men's, rather than women's, mentalities, we have focused, thus far,
on claims concerning women's and men's mentalities. Suppose, however,
that the critiques I have suggested are incorrect. I believe that this argument for the androcentricity of philosophy still fails, since it also characterizes *philosophy* in a problematic way.

   Take, for example, claims about the character of ethics. Many philosophers influenced by Gilligan's work have characterized most of ethics as
justice ethics, thus suggesting that it does not agree well with women's
minds, and hence that an alternative, feminine ethics is required. Nel
Noddings, for example, writes in her *Caring: A Feminine Approach to
Ethics and Moral Education* that

> ethics, the philosophical study of morality, has concentrated for
> the most part on moral reasoning . . . ethical argumentation has
> frequently proceeded as if it were governed by the logical neces-
> sity characteristic of geometry. It has concentrated on the estab-
> lishment of principles and that which can be logically derived
> from them. One might say that ethics has been discussed largely
> in the language of the father: in principles and propositions, in
> terms such as justification, fairness, justice . . . . One is tempted

25. Hartsock's view on the tenability of biological arguments is somewhat unclear,
since she also writes: "Let me state explicitly that I do not believe this is a biological distinction at all, since a number of men . . . have put forward theories that take fundamentally
similar positions [to women's]." *Money, Sex and Power,* 15 n. 22.

to say that ethics has so far been guided by Logos, the masculine spirit. (1)

Likewise, Nancy Tuana writes that

> feminists are working on similar transformations of moral theories. . . . Feminists argue that the basic categories of moral theory lead to a definition of moral competence as masculine; that is, the moral agent is perceived as male. Thus traditional ethical theory is seen as insufficient to address the concerns and experiences of women. Rather than attempt to argue that women are capable of full moral agency as traditionally defined, feminist ethicists are working to reconstruct moral theory. Traditional moral theory is criticized for positing a conception of people as disinterested, independent individuals, who are both free and equals, and of a moral agent as impartial. Many feminist theorists argue instead for a model of moral thinking based on relationships, with moral actions arising out of responsibilities and affiliations rather than duties or rights.
>
> Currently the most influential of these alternative models of morality is what has been labeled an "ethics of care" . . . an ethics of care replaces the autonomous moral agent who uses reason to understand and apply a set of universal moral rules with the member of a community who responds to others in a caring way that aims to prevent harm and to sustain relationships. . . . It is believed that such transformations of ethical theory will both acknowledge the experiences of women and include issues of special concern to women, both of which are neglected in traditional ethical theory.[26]

I believe, however, that an examination of the history of ethics shows that neither all nor most of Western ethical theories have only or largely the characteristics of justice ethics. Some traditional ethics are characterized by what Noddings calls the "language of the mother." Albert Camus's ethics, for example, calls for an immediate and nonrational empathy.[27] Buber's I-Thou attitude is also relational, contextual, immediate, nonprocedural, addressed to unique subjects in concrete situations,

26. *Woman and the History of Philosophy,* 118–19.
27. See, for example, *The Plague.*

and does not separate emotion from intellect. In contrast, the I-It attitude, where others are subsumed under general laws instead of being attended to as unique, is closer to justice ethics.[28] Nor are the basic principles of care ethics very different from those preached by Jesus in the Gospel. Jesus, too, propounds concrete, contextual, and immediate empathy toward others. His proposal, too, is not based on laws and procedures, nor on a separation between emotion and intellect. Annette C. Baier shows the affinity of Gilligan's care ethics to Hume's moral theory, and Joan C. Tronto points out its affinity to the moral theories of Hutcheson and the common sense moralists in general.[29] Other ethical teachings present admixtures of "justice characteristics" and "care characteristics," corresponding, perhaps, to what Gilligan has in mind when she suggests, at the end of her book, some kind of a combination of what she calls care ethics and justice ethics.[30] Aristotle's ethic does not incorporate much care for others, but it is mostly nonprocedural (except for his discussion of the practical syllogisms), and is nonuniversalistic, imprecise, and contextual. The moral teachings of the Stoics also combine elements of justice and care ethics,[31] as do some medieval Christian ethics, which integrate discussions of empathy, love, and *caritas* (caring, empathy, and devotion to others and God, sometimes problematically translated in English as "charity") with other religious teachings. Thus Jean Bethke Elshtain, for example, shows how Augustine's understanding of the notions of *imago Dei* and pride relate to empathy.[32] Likewise, Aquinas believes that Christian perfection consists in loving others as ourselves and in loving God.[33] Nor can the moral theories of the modern era be characterized as pure justice ethics. Spinoza presents his moral theory as intellectual, objective, and universal, but at the same time also as emotional and

28. See Buber, *I and Thou.*

29. Baier, "Hume, The Women's Moral Theorist?"; Tronto, "Political Science and Caring."

30. *In a Different Voice,* 174.

31. See, for example, Seneca, *On Anger* and *On Mercy.*

32. See Elshtain, "Augustine and Diversity." See also Augustine's "What arguments, what works of any philosophers, what laws of any states can be compared in any way with the two commandments . . . 'Thou shalt love the Lord thy God with thy whole heart . . . ; and thou shalt love thy neighbor as thyself' . . . herein is ethics, since the good and honorable life is formed in no other way than by loving what ought to be loved as it ought to be loved, that is, God and our neighbor." Letter 137, in *Saint Augustine: Letters,* vol. 3, trans. Wilfrid Parsons, The Fathers of the Church Series, vol. 20 (Washington, D.C.: The Catholic University of America Press, 1953), 33–34.

33. *Summa Theologica* IIa IIae q. 184 a. 3. See also *Summa Theologica* IIa IIae qq. 23–33 (esp. q. 23 a. 6 and a. 8).

nonprocedural. The moral teachings of the Romantics are also far from being justice ethics, as are those of existentialists such as Kierkegaard, Sartre, or Gabriel Marcel. It seems that many of the scholars who discuss justice ethics think of the moral theories of Kant, Mill, and philosophers who are influenced by them such as Rawls. It is important to remember, however, that these do not constitute the majority of moral thinking. (Moreover, as Susan Moller Okin, Onora O'Neill, and Robert B. Louden have shown, not all of these authors can be considered as pure "justice" moralists.)[34] Significant parts of the history of ethics, then, do not display justice characteristics. Thus, they do not suit, or reflect, what are taken to be men's mentalities rather than women's.

Similar problems, I believe, beset other suggestions. Merrill B. Hintikka and Jaakko Hintikka's representation of philosophy is also problematic. According to them, "it is arguable that Western philosophical thought has been overemphasizing such ontological models as postulate a given fixed supply of discrete individuals, individuated by their intrinsic or essential (non-relational) properties."[35] They find such bias in recent philosophical semantics and ontology, as well as in the history of philosophy. For example, "separability and 'thisness' were the characteristic marks of Aristotelian substances, which are historically the most important proposed ontological units of the world. Conversely, we may very well ask whether Leibniz's ontology of monads, whose identity lies in their reflecting the whole universe, has really been given its due" (147). This accords well with what they take to be boys' and men's tendency to prefer discrete and manipulatable units. (Girls and women, on the other hand, are taken to view the world in more relational and functional ways.)[36] However, this seems problematic. Although Aristotelian substances are indeed separable, they are related to each other, and Aristotle's worldview is functional. On the other hand, although each of Leibniz's monads reflects all the others and the whole universe, and although all their changes are ordered by a preestablished harmony, the monads are distinct and separable substances that cannot causally inter-

---

34. For Rawls, see Okin, "Reason and Feeling." For Kant, see O'Neill, "Kant After Virtue," and Louden, "Kant's Virtue Ethics." Note that Mill's theory, too, incorporates caring for others' happiness and well-being, and leaves room for a degree of subjectivism by deciding what enhances happiness according to one's own liking.

35. "How Can Language Be Sexist?" 146.

36. However, Hintikka and Hintikka are cautious and qualify their claims, as in "the suggestion—and we do not intend it to be more than a suggestion—we make here is now clear: it is not just possible, but quite likely that there are sex-linked differences in our processes of cross-identification" (146).

act with each other in any way. Both models, then, combine elements of distinctness and interrelation, and the differences between them in these respects are less sharp than may at first appear. And there are many other models in the history of philosophy that combine relation and distinctness in different forms and to different degrees, such as those of Hegel and the Hegelians, or those that compare society, the state, or the universe to an organism.[37] It is not clear how these views should be ranked in terms of "distinctness of entities" versus "relatedness of entities."

Similar problems arise for Hartsock's argument. Hartsock qualifies her suggestion, pointing out that "several cases clearly constitute only suggestive evidence for my argument."[38] Yet, she suggests that men's and women's discussions of power differ, in that "theories of power put forward by women rather than men differ systematically from the understanding of power as domination" (210). While she "was unable to discover any woman writing about power who did not stress those aspects of power related to energy, capacity, and potential" (ibid.), men who write about power present it as more related to hegemony or confrontation. Moreover,

> my argument for the genderedness of current understandings of power gains additional support from the fact that when women (not necessarily feminists) write about power, they put forward accounts that are both strikingly similar to each other and strikingly different from those of the men considered in this book. Indeed, one can almost argue that there is a separate and distinct women's tradition of theorizing power. (151)

This seems to me incorrect. Most male political theorists, too, do not see political power only in terms of domination and control. Liberal, socialist, Marxist, pacifist, and anarchist political theorists frequently discuss the injustice and domination in the social political frameworks they criti-

---

37. See, for example, Plato *Timaeus* 30b–31b; *Republic* V 462c–e; Aristotle *Politics* 1253a 20–25; Seneca *On Anger* II 31, 7; Marcus Aurelius *Meditations* VII, 13; Cicero *On Duties* (*De officiis*) III 21; Aquinas *Summa Theologica* IIIa q. 8 a. 3; Friedrich Wilhelm Joseph Schelling, *Von der Weltseele, eine Hypothese der höhren Physik zur Erklärung des allgemeinen Organismus*, in *Schriften von 1794–98*, vol. 4 of *Schelling: Ausgewählte Werke* (J. G. Cotta'scher Verlag edition, Stuttgart and Augsburg, 1856–57; reprint, Darmstadt: Wissenschaftliche Buchgesellschaft, 1967), p. 554 [500]; Herbert Spencer, *The Principles of Sociology* (London: Williams and Norgate, 1897–1906; reprint, Westport, Conn.: Greenwood Press, 1974), vol. 1, pt. 2, sec. 2.

38. *Money, Sex and Power*, 210.

cize, but analyze power as related to consent, cooperation, ability, energy, and growth in the social-political frameworks that they call for. And a significant number of feminist authors do stress aspects of power that are related to confrontation and domination much more than to capacity, potential, or energy. Rather than taking phenomena usually seen as confrontational and presenting them as nonconfrontational, they take phenomena usually seen as nonconfrontational (for example, visual art, literature, family life, romance, sex) and explain many aspects of them in terms of domination and hegemony.[39] Many of the feminist arguments discussed in this book are also examples of seeing a field traditionally understood as unrelated to hegemony and domination, namely philosophy, and arguing that it is significantly informed by such categories.[40]

It is also interesting in this context to examine claims concerning the aggressiveness of philosophy. A widely cited discussion of this topic is Janice Moulton's "A Paradigm of Philosophy: The Adversary Method." Moulton does not commit herself to the claim that men are more aggressive than women (12) and criticizes what she terms "the adversary method" for other, independent reasons. However, her paper is important in the context of the present discussion because of her contention that much of the philosophical practice follows the adversary method (or paradigm), and thus is aggressive.

Moulton takes the adversary method, which matches Karl Popper's conjectures and refutations model, to be "a model of philosophic methodology that accepts a positive view of aggressive behavior and uses it as a paradigm of philosophic reasoning" (11). Moreover, she believes that this method is highly prevalent in philosophical discussions of recent decades, and that it "dominates the methodology and evaluation of philosophy" (15). This has had negative consequences for philosophical discussion, and hence Moulton believes that the adversary paradigm should be supplemented or replaced by other types of reasoning. As she describes it, according to the adversary model

> all philosophic reasoning is, or ought to be, deductive. General claims are made and the job of philosophic research is to find counterexamples to the claims. And most important, the philo-

---

39. This attitude is also expressed in the popular slogan "The personal is political."

40. Cf. Elshtain's discussion of Susan Brownmiller, Mary Daly, and some radical feminist descriptions of the social world, in her "Feminist Discourse and Its Discontents," 610–11, as well as Elshtain's discussion of various feminist conceptions of war and conflict in "Ethics in the Women's Movement," 238–39.

sophic enterprise is seen as an unimpassioned debate between *adversaries* who try to defend their own views against counterexamples and produce counterexamples to opposing views. (14; Moulton's emphasis)

Moulton also argues that "philosophers who cannot be recast into an adversarial mold are likely to be ignored" (17). This may be the reason "why Emerson, Carlyle and others are discussed only as part of English literature, and their views are not studied much by philosophers. They are not addressing adversaries, but merely presenting a system of ideas" (24 n. 9).

However, I do not think that the model Moulton describes has indeed come to dominate the methodology and evaluation of philosophy (including analytic philosophy of recent decades). For all its interest and power, Popper's conjectures and refutations model has not been widely accepted or followed in philosophy (or in science). When deductions or use of counterexamples are found, they are frequently supplemented by other modes of reasoning, just as Moulton thinks they should.

It may be suggested, however, that the gist of Moulton's argument does not have to do specifically with Popper's conjectures and refutations model, but with philosophical criticism, debate, argumentation, and disagreement in general. Thus her critique does apply to philosophy in the past few decades, moreover to much of philosophical practice at large. However, disagreement, argumentation, debate, and criticism are not inherently aggressive. Parties to philosophical disagreements or debates need not be adversaries. Philosophical criticism may indeed be presented in an aggressive style, but this aggressiveness is not part and parcel of the criticism, and we can reject the aggressiveness while retaining debate and argumentation. Of course, the importance of considering the evidence for and against the view one holds, relative to its alternatives, cannot be overemphasized. It is philosophically (and humanly) worthy not to accept or reject a view at face value, or just because someone mentioned it, or because it is popular, or is unpopular, and so on, but to try to explain to oneself and to others why a certain view seems to one preferable to alternatives, and to inquire seriously whether it is indeed so, after carefully considering others' arguments for their views.

But it may also be suggested that Moulton's argument should be read as making claims not about the *inherent* aggressiveness of Popperian or other philosophical argumentation or disagreement, but about the *actual* aggressive style that philosophical discussions sometimes assume. This aggressiveness is indeed unpleasant (and counterproductive). But it is not a frequent phenomenon in most philosophical texts; most of them are not written in an aggressive style. Oral discussions, too, become aggressive from time to time, and do so, it seems, more than written discussions; yet in most cases they too are polite or even cordial (without being sarcastically polite or cordial). Some very unpleasant and well-remembered exceptions notwithstanding, most written and oral philosophical discussions are carried out in a straightforward rather than a debasing way, and views, arguments, and corrections are presented as a matter of fact, without by-messages that aim to humiliate or otherwise hurt the other side.

It is important, of course, not to confuse assertiveness with aggression, in either direction. Realizing that one has made a mistake, or that the view one has accepted is more problematic than alternatives, can be emotionally unpleasant. Thus, the argumentation that shows this to one may be experienced as aggressive even when it is merely assertive. On the other hand, there are cases where the evaluation of the evidence for different views, which requires also a clear discussion of some weaknesses in evidence and argumentation, is used as an alibi for treating others belligerently and in a humiliating manner. Both of these aberrations do sometimes appear in philosophy, and both should be avoided.

6

We have seen in the previous sections that the argument from the parallels between the characteristics of philosophy and the characteristics of men's, rather than women's, mentalities, is problematic in a number of ways. But there is a further difficulty in this argument. Even those who believe that women's and men's mentalities differ significantly do not take the mentalities to be complete, pure opposites (although they are sometimes popularly represented that way). Gilligan, for example, takes both women's and men's mentalities to combine justice characteristics with care characteristics. True, women's "blend" of care characteristics and justice characteristics is taken to have more of the former than men's "blend," but both genders combine both sets of characteristics. Hintikka and Hintikka too are clear that what they take to be feminine and masculine characteristics can be found in both men and women, and talk only of stronger tendencies or emphases. Hartsock too would surely not deny that women have a fair proportion of the characteristics she attributes to men, even if to a lesser degree, and that men have a fair proportion of the characteristics she attributes to women, even if to a lesser degree. The differences (if they exist) are of degree, not of kind.

Philosophical theories, too, show a "blend" of care characteristics and justice characteristics, or of Hintikka and Hintikka's "relationality" and "separateness," and so on. Yet if this is so, I do not see how can it be proved (except for very radical cases) that a certain philosophical "blend" of, say, care characteristics and justice characteristics, agrees with, or reflects, specifically men's "blend" of these characteristics rather than women's. It is very difficult to show that a certain philosophical "blend" of, say, Hintikka and Hintikka's "relationality" and "separateness" suits or reflects men's rather than women's mental "blend" of these characteristics. The same is true of the other authors mentioned in this chapter.

I suggest, then, that even if the argument examined in this chapter were not problematic both in how it represents men's and women's mentalities, and in how it represents philosophy, it would have remained difficult to corroborate the claim that a certain philosophical combination is analogous not to women's combination of "feminine" and "masculine" characteristics, but rather to men's. For this reason too, then, the argument from the parallels between philosophy and men's, rather than women's, mentalities, seems unhelpful.

8

Androcentric Omissions

I

Some authors point out not only what philosophers have said about women but also what they have failed to say. For example, various philosophers have failed to discuss, in contexts where such discussions would have been relevant, issues pertaining mainly to women's experiences (for example, sexual harassment or abortion). Similarly, many philosophers have failed to criticize, in contexts where this would have been pertinent, how women have suffered from various sorts of discrimination. Until such omissions are rectified, it is argued, the theories remain, in this respect, androcentric. I believe that in some cases these claims are correct. Arguments by omission can be presented in the following form:

1. A philosophy (or philosophy at large) refrains from discussing issues relating to women in a context where such a discussion is appropriate and relevant.
2. Conclusion: The philosophy (or philosophy at large) suits men's experiences or minds more than women's, or involves discrimination against women; that is, the philosophy (or philosophy at large) is androcentric.

The androcentricity of omission, too, can be pervasive or nonpervasive. If the addenda needed to rectify the omission are inconsistent with many parts of the theory, to the extent that the latter have to be rejected, replaced, or radically changed, the androcentricity is pervasive. If, on the other hand, the needed addenda are not inconsistent with any part of the theory, so that none of its claims would have to be rejected, replaced, or changed; or if the addenda are inconsistent with only a few of the theses of the theory, and thus call for only a few changes, the androcentricity is nonpervasive. To decide whether the androcentricity of an omission is pervasive or nonpervasive, then, one needs to examine the existing parts of the theory, and to estimate whether, or to what extent, they are in conflict with the necessary addenda. The remedial addenda may be in conflict, for example, with prior androcentric themes in the theory. Hence, measuring the pervasiveness of the androcentricity of an omission may require examining whether other, already existing parts of the theory are androcentric, and if so, to what extent. This undertaking may involve discussions of the theory in general, and of the androcentricity of its parts; such discussions would resemble those in previous chapters concerning the androcentricity of philosophical systems.

To accept that a work has omitted discussion of a certain notion, it must be agreed that discussing that notion is within the purpose and scope of that work. Works cannot, and should not be expected to, discuss all issues from all perspectives. Each work has its own scope and purpose, and not discussing an issue that is not within that scope is not an omission. To take an obvious example, a work on Locke's theory of causation is not in omission for not discussing carpentry in Babylon in the second millennium B.C.E. But neither is it at fault for not discussing Plotinus's Nous or Hegel's Dialectic. The scope of a philosophical work is also determined by its length and by the degree of detail for which it strives. A very short history of Western philosophy would be in omission for not discussing Kant, but not for failing to discuss one of the lesser Peripatetics. It would be in omission for not discussing Hegel, but less so, or not so at all, for not discussing some of the young Hegelians. Philosophical orientation is also relevant. Many analytic philosophers, for example, are not interested in building systems, but see themselves more as puzzle solvers dealing with specific problems. Thus, silence concerning a certain issue might not be an omission in an analytic work yet might be an omission in a Continental-systematic one. In judgments about omissions, then, much depends on our understanding of the scope and nature of the works in question.

Arguments by omission are not frequent in feminist philosophical literature, and have been developed by only a few feminist philosophers. I will examine examples of their use by two scholars, Lorraine Code, concerning positivist epistemology, and Susan Moller Okin, concerning political theory. Some uses of this argument, I will suggest, do not show philosophy to be either pervasively or nonpervasively androcentric. Others show it to be nonpervasively androcentric; but none shows it to be pervasively so.

2

Lorraine Code argues that epistemology does not discuss questions such as who can have knowledge, and who (such as, for example, women on welfare) cannot. Thus, in a chapter called "Remapping the Epistemic Terrain," she writes that "the epistemic terrain is mapped out so that the welfare women can pose no problem." Moreover,

> as the map [of the "epistemic terrain"] is currently drawn, there is no place for analyses of the availability of knowledge, of knowledge acquisition processes, or—above all—of the political considerations that are implicated in knowing anything more interesting than the fact that the cup is not the table, now.[1]

Furthermore,

> I have examined some of these mechanisms [of power and politics] and assumptions in this book to demonstrate their alignment both with the androcentricity of epistemology and with the effectiveness of established epistemologies in serving white, privileged, masculine interests. Feminists who expect a theory of knowledge to address people's everyday cognitive experiences and to examine the place of knowledge in people's lives, who expect it to produce analyses and strategies that will contribute to the construction of a world fit for human habitation, can find little enlightenment in mainstream epistemology. (267)

I suggest, however, that the field I refer to here, rather imprecisely, as "analytic epistemology" is not in omission for not discussing these topics, since they are not within its scope. The topics Code mentions are dealt with in the sociology of knowledge, social epistemology, and works related to Marxist, Foucauldian, and the Frankfurt School traditions. Analytic epistemology is a field with its own scope and subject matter,

---

1. *What Can She Know?* 266.

just as is the sociology of knowledge, and it need not be criticized for not dealing with issues outside its scope. Just as one would not expect a study of the influence of economic considerations on the acquisition of knowledge to digress and discuss whether knowledge is indeed justified true belief, one should not expect a study of the latter issue—also a legitimate subject of thought and research—to digress into a discussion concerning the former. There may be some contexts in which the two should be discussed conjointly, but there are also others in which they should be discussed independently. Many works have been published on the former issue, and many on the latter. None of these themes is overly neglected.

Assume, however, that analytic epistemology should have discussed, or should have discussed more extensively, issues in the sociology of knowledge (or social epistemology). Would this omission be pervasive or nonpervasive? The latter, I believe. The discussion of themes in analytic epistemology does not preclude the discussion of themes in the sociology of knowledge, and many of the methodologies employed in analytic epistemology can also be used to discuss issues in the sociology of knowledge. Following the methodological presuppositions of analytic epistemology, there would be an effort to discuss issues in sociology of knowledge with clarity and precision, to examine carefully what conclusions the evidence supports, and so on. But these surely are standards that most scholars would embrace.

3

Susan Moller Okin applies the argument by omission to political theory. She writes that

> political theory, which had been sparse for a period before the late 1960s except as an important branch of intellectual history, has become a flourishing field, with social justice as its central concern. Yet, remarkably, major contemporary theorists of justice have almost without exception . . . displayed little interest in or knowledge of the findings of feminism. They have largely bypassed the fact that the society to which their theories are supposed to pertain is heavily and deeply affected by gender, and faces difficult issues of justice stemming from its gendered past and present assumptions.[2]

2. *Justice, Gender and the Family,* 7–8.

Okin also argues that contemporary political theories, or theories of justice, "persist, despite the wealth of the feminist challenges to their assumptions, in their refusal even to discuss the family and its gender structure" (9).[3] She comments on a large number of authors as well as on the field in general, but analyzes in detail specific works of seven thinkers: Alan Bloom, Alasdair MacIntyre, Robert Nozick, Michael Sandel, John Rawls, Michael Walzer, and Roberto Unger. Of the seven theories, Okin considers three to be pervasively androcentric: Bloom's, MacIntyre's, and Nozick's. Two other theories are presented as nonpervasively androcentric: Rawls's and Walzer's. Okin does not specify whether she takes Sandel's theory to be pervasively androcentric, and her discussion suggests that she does not take Unger's to be so. For reasons of space, I cannot discuss all of Okin's analyses here, and will focus on those with which I disagree the most, namely, those concerning two of the theories that she takes to be pervasively androcentric (MacIntyre's and Nozick's), and the one that she might consider as such (Sandel's).[4] Okin also sometimes mentions points where the authors she discusses are guilty of androcentricity by commission; I will focus here, however, on the issue of androcentricity by omission.

Okin also presents some general claims about contemporary political theories in her introduction. She believes that the failure of contemporary political theories to sufficiently discuss gender justice and family justice issues is related to their acceptance of both the public-domestic dichotomy and the notion that the domestic sphere is outside the scope of their discussion (9).[5] Moreover, contemporary political theories apply only to half of us, assume that "half of us take care of whole areas of life that are considered outside the scope of social justice" (15), and do not treat women as "full human beings to whom a theory of social justice must apply" (23). She does not specify whether she takes these general

3. Some may believe that issues of gender justice and family justice should be discussed within moral rather than political theory, and hence claim that refraining from discussing these issues within political theory is not an omission. Since this book discusses questions of androcentricity in philosophy in general, it is not important in this context where precisely the asserted omissions occur.

4. Although Okin's analysis suggests that Bloom's *Closing of the American Mind* is also pervasively androcentric, I have chosen not to consider it here. Okin's general thesis is about contemporary political theories or justice theories; and although Bloom is, of course, a political theorist, I believe that most scholars, including Bloom himself, would not have considered this book of his as a work in political theory or justice theory.

5. Okin prefers "public-domestic" to the more common "public-private," since the latter is ambiguous (*Justice, Gender and the Family*, 198 n. 1). I follow her usage here.

claims about contemporary political theory to be true of all the theories upon which she elaborates, and if not, of which ones they are true.[6] Hence, I examine these general claims in relation to each of the three theories discussed ahead. I suggest that the claims are true of none.

4

Okin examines Alasdair MacIntyre's views as they appear in his *After Virtue* and the later *Whose Justice? Which Rationality?* She describes how MacIntyre believes that familiarizing ourselves with certain traditions would help us to reach a better general understanding of justice, as well as better decisions concerning specific issues. According to him, liberal thinkers have failed to give satisfactory answers to many problems, or to present coherent and satisfying understandings of the nature of morality and justice. While liberals have called for detaching ourselves from particular standpoints, MacIntyre wants us, on the contrary, to adopt particular points of view, or orientations, when we think and decide about moral-political issues. He relies mainly on the traditions of Classical Greece (where he reserves an especially important place for Aristotle), and on Christian traditions, particularly the Augustinian-Calvinist and Thomist (46).

Okin argues that MacIntyre does not devote enough space to issues of gender and family justice. Moreover, she claims, he frequently avoids discussing in sufficient detail the misogynous elements in the traditions that he recommends. For example, when speaking of Aristotle's ideal of the good life, MacIntyre employs gender-neutral language and does not point out, or does not point out sufficiently, that Aristotle reserved this ideal for men (53–55). He also hardly mentions the conditions of Homeric women when he describes the values of that period (49–50). Likewise, "in the context of the Adam and Eve story and Augustine's conception of the will, MacIntyre persistently employs gender-neutral language, even though Christian (especially Catholic) theology has assigned to Eve the primary blame for the fall from grace" (45). He also ignores Augustine's claim that women are naturally subordinate to men (57), and disregards Aquinas's view of women as misbegotten men (58).

---

6. Except for the last claim, about treating women as "full human beings to whom a theory of social justice must apply," which is taken to be true of all the theories, even if some of them, "though unsatisfactory as they stand, have considerable potential for the development of a fully humanist theory of justice" (ibid., 23).

While MacIntyre does discuss the family, he does not observe that women have contributed most to rearing children, and does not emphasize the virtues related to this work, without which there would have been no people to live the good or virtuous life (56).

Some of these criticisms seem to me problematic. For example, although MacIntyre does not mention that Eve is the temptress in the story of the Fall, I believe that in the context of his discussion he does not need to do so. His purpose in that discussion is to follow the historical emergence of the notion of the will. Thus, he describes how, for Plato and Aristotle, reason incorporated inclination or disinclination toward what one is thinking about. Augustine, however, separated reason, on the one hand, and inclination (or will), on the other, believing that "intellect itself needs to be moved to activity by will" (*Whose Justice?* 156). According to Augustine, however, from the time of the Original Sin the will has been unable to direct itself. Because "Adam chose to direct his will to the love of self rather than of God . . . [he] impaired his freedom to choose good . . . [and] from then on lacked any resources to recover that freedom" (157). Thus, people can be redeemed from this condition only through divine grace, and by freely consenting to receive it. One consequence of this is that we need humility if we wish our character to be informed by justice (ibid.). Another is that we should acknowledge our freedom. There are also other implications. MacIntyre indeed does not point out, in the context of this discussion, that "Christian (especially Catholic) theology has assigned to Eve the primary blame for the fall from grace."[7] But this is irrelevant to his discussion. His silence concerning Eve's part in the story is not, in this context, an omission. Likewise, when MacIntyre refers to Aristotle's *anthropos* as "he or she," he most probably is not trying to give a false impression, but rather to suggest that what he takes to be worthy in the traditions he discusses is relevant

7. This claim about Christianity's (especially Catholicism's) tendency to assign to Eve the primary blame for the fall from grace may be untrue of Augustine. As Jean Bethke Elshtain shows, for Augustine "Adam and Eve . . . are both responsible for the entry of sin into the world. Augustine's story of the fall is a story of the 'first human beings.' His reference point is 'they'—they 'did not deny their sin . . . their pride seeks to pin the wrong act on another; the woman's pride blames the serpent, the man's pride blames the woman.' Both allowed themselves to be tempted. Both committed offenses. Both tried to pass the buck." Elshtain, *Augustine and the Limits of Politics*, 44. (Okin does present Augustine's other nuanced views on women and men on p. 57 of *Justice, Gender and the Family*.) I do not press this matter here, however, since the issue at hand is whether, *if* Okin is correct and Elshtain wrong, MacIntyre should have dealt in this specific discussion with Eve's supposedly greater responsibility for the fall.

to both genders, since he does discuss Aristotle's androcentric claims, analyzes the fallacious reasoning behind them, and suggests that this bias should be corrected (*Whose Justice?* 104–5).

Some of Okin's other criticisms, however, are correct, and it seems that in various instances MacIntyre should have written, or should have written more elaborately, on the androcentric views in the traditions he discusses, as well as have devoted more space to issues of family justice and gender justice. But if discussions of such issues were to be added to his theory, very little else, if anything, would need changing. Thus, if these omissions make MacIntyre's theory androcentric, they make it non-pervasively so. Okin, however, argues that MacIntyre is pervasively androcentric. She points out that "it is by now obvious that many of 'our' traditions, and certainly those evaluated most highly by MacIntyre, are so permeated by the patriarchal power structure within which they evolved as to require nothing less than radical and intensive challenge if they are to meet truly humanist conceptions of the virtues" (*Justice, Gender, and the Family*, 58). It is for this reason that she takes the imposition of egalitarianism on his theory to completely demolish it (23), and refers to MacIntyre as a "reactionary" (117). This is also apparent in many of her specific objections, which point out androcentric passages in Aristotle, Augustine, and Aquinas, and argue that these also incriminate MacIntyre's endeavor (for example, 55, 59). However, as recounted— but insufficiently noted, I believe—by Okin herself (for example, 47–48, 58), the great majority of MacIntyre's descriptions of the way we should employ traditions, and especially the way he does so himself, show that he adopts a dynamic and critical approach, rather than a passive one. He frequently suggests that although traditions should be heeded and used, they should not be accepted fully, literally, and uncritically. He emphasizes that there is much room—as well as need—for interpretation and reinterpretation, adaptation, and reworking, much of which is subjective (*After Virtue*, 111, 137, 149, 170, 241; *Whose Justice?* ix, 85, 327, 389–403). His position thus can be compared to that of many Muslims, Christians, Jews, and followers of other faiths, some of them feminists, who neither follow nor reject *all* that is found in their tradition. Although these believers do not conform to every single aspect of their heritage, they find much of it to be important and valuable, and wish to develop their own attitudes in relation to these aspects. Thus, they subscribe to traditions, but not wholly, or blindly, or without taking other considerations into account. It would have indeed been impossible for MacIntyre to accept literally and in detail all the traditions he draws from, even if only because these traditions differ on so many issues.

Okin also comments on a contradiction she finds in MacIntyre: "He gives conflicting accounts of what a tradition *is*. At times he describes it as a defining context, stressing the authoritative nature of its 'texts'; at times he talks of a tradition as 'living,' as a 'not-yet-completed narrative,' as an argument about the goods that constitute the tradition" (*Justice, Gender, and the Family*, 61; Okin's emphasis). However, as I have suggested, these need not be conflicting accounts, since seeing traditions as defining contexts and as having some authority does not preclude viewing them as living and still incomplete.

There is another omission in MacIntyre's theory Okin points at: he fails to address many specific matters of importance to women. She argues that a contemporary young woman in the United States, for example, would not find the traditions on which MacIntyre relies helpful in deciding how to balance her family life and work (59). However, MacIntyre intends to discuss only general principles, and he leaves the reflection and decision about many of the specifics open for those who want to enter into dialogue with the traditions he discusses (or others). Hence he hardly addresses in these writings any specific moral and political questions; these are outside the scope and intention of his discussion.

Do Okin's general criticisms of modern political theories, in the introduction to her book, apply to MacIntyre's theory? Again, it is not clear to which of the theories Okin discusses the criticisms are meant to apply, but if they are directed at MacIntyre's work, they seem incorrect. Although MacIntyre does omit the discussion of some gender or family justice issues, it is unlikely that this omission is related to a belief that these issues lie beyond the scope of his discussion, since, as Okin too points out (56), he does discuss the family. Nor is it correct to characterize MacIntyre's theory as applying only to half of us. In all or almost all the issues it treats, the theory applies to both women and men. Nor does MacIntyre see women as less than full human beings, or assume that only half of us would be responsible for the domestic sphere.

5

Okin argues that Robert Nozick's *Anarchy, State and Utopia* is another moral-political theory flawed by androcentric omission. Moreover, she contends that its androcentricity is pervasive:

> Focusing mainly on the work of the most influential of contem-
> porary academic libertarians, Robert Nozick, I conclude that
> this theory is reduced to absurdity when women are taken into
> account. Instead of the minimal state that he argues for in *Anar-
> chy, State and Utopia,* what results is a bizarre combination of
> matriarchy and slavery that all would probably agree is better
> described as *dystopia.* (75; see also 76n; Okin's emphasis)

Okin also claims that if egalitarianism were imposed upon Nozick's theory, it would be completely demolished (23). I will argue that although
there are some androcentric omissions in the theory, they make it nonpervasively rather than pervasively androcentric.

While Okin is critical of Nozick's theory for other reasons as well, she
ignores such criticisms for the sake of argument (75; see also 76n). As
described by Okin, Nozick calls for a minimal state and is highly critical
of taxation and welfare. Negative property rights are seen as primary
and override even positive life rights: "Nozick claims that individuals'
entitlements to things they own take precedence over any other rights,
even the right to basic subsistence" (77). An important way of becoming
entitled to something is to produce it, if the resources used in the process
of production have been contracted for or bought (78). Moreover, the
theory presupposes that people own themselves; otherwise the entitlement theory would become problematic (79–80). Okin points out, however, that this involves Nozick in a difficulty. Children are "produced"
by their mothers. According to the logic of Nozick's argument, this suggests that children (and when they grow up, adults) also belong to their
mothers.[8] Accordingly, mothers may do whatever they please with their
children, including treating them as slaves or selling them into slavery.
The emerging situation is clearly untenable: it is a state of slavery for all
(except those freed by their mothers or by other owners). Mothers would
have enormous power, and we would have "a "matriarchy" of a sort
no more appealing to feminists than to antifeminists." This would be a
"dystopia," rather than utopia, or even a bearable situation. Moreover,

> the immediate problem of this analysis for Nozick . . . is that it
> leaves the core of his theory—the principle of acquisition—mired
> in self-contradiction. If persons do not even "own" themselves,

---

8. I am not sure Okin's discussion pays sufficient attention to the role of fathers in
"producing" children, but will ignore this issue here.

in the sense of being entitled to their own persons, bodies, natural talents, abilities, and so on, then there would appear to be no basis for anyone's owning anything else. Nozick's theory of entitlement is clearly premised on the notion that each person owns himself. (86).

Okin believes that this difficulty reduces Nozick's theory to absurdity. However, Nozick offers some characteristics that impose constraints on how people may treat each other. Although he accepts slavery, he also writes, as Okin notes, that there are choices individuals may make for themselves, but others may not make for them (Nozick, *Anarchy, State and Utopia,* 331; Okin, *Justice, Gender, and the Family,* 81). This may rule out slavery of the type Okin discusses, namely, a slavery into which one is born, without choosing it, simply since one was "produced" by parents. Perhaps, however, Nozick does not think that entering into slavery is one of those choices that individuals may make for themselves, but others may not make for them (although he does point out that "some things individuals may choose for themselves, no one may choose for another" immediately after discussing selling oneself into slavery). If this is accepted, the theory is indeed problematic and needs to be changed. It could easily be modified, however, by introducing into it, for example, the claim just mentioned, namely, that one can become a slave only by freely choosing to be so. Or it could be changed by disallowing in it any type of slavery. Changing the theory in such limited ways would solve the problem Okin points out, without completely demolishing it, as she argues is necessary.

This addresses what Okin takes to be the central androcentric problem in Nozick's theory, which she relates to his apparent failure to consider family and children. However, she points out other omissions in Nozick's and other libertarians' theories as well:

> Reformers' arguments about just allocations of property and income after divorce have raised the fundamental question of what is and what is not to be regarded as reproductive labor, deserving of monetary reward. And the struggle over comparable worth has raised the added complexity of how different types of productivity, commonly divided along sex lines, *within* the realm of wage work are to be measured against one another so that they can be justly compensated. Libertarian theorists have not been accustomed to addressing such questions. Like almost all politi-

cal theorists, whether explicitly or implicitly, they have assumed as their subject matter the male heads of families. But what happens when we question this assumption? (75–76; Okin's emphasis)

Moreover,

[children] need years and years of attentive care, at least some of which needs to be provided by persons who love them and know them very well—in most cases, their parents. Nozick's theory is able to ignore this fact of life, and childhood in general, only by assuming that women, in families, continue to do their work of nurturing and socializing the young and of providing a sphere of intimate relations. As we are finding to be so often the case, the family and a large part of the lives of most women, especially, are assumed by the theory but are not part of it in the important sense of having its conclusions applied to them. (87)

Issues of education and raising children, as well as of family and gender justice in general, are indeed frequently not discussed, or not discussed in sufficient detail, in libertarian theories. But a Nozickian might answer that such omissions could easily be rectified, and hence the androcentricity in the theory is nonpervasive. Okin also claims that libertarians "have assumed as their subject matter the male heads of families" (75–76). I suggest, however, that this claim is not justified by the evidence. Although libertarians should probably devote more consideration to issues of gender justice and family justice, all or almost all of what they write applies to both men and women. Okin's criticism would have been correct if women owned no property, never signed contracts, were never taxed, and so on. The same is true of the claim that Nozick can ignore some issues in family justice "*only* by assuming that women, in families, continue to do their work of nurturing and socializing the young and of providing a sphere of intimate relations" (87; my emphasis). But this is not the *only* possible explanation for Nozick's relative silence about family justice issues. As Roy Perrett notes (in a discussion that focuses on other issues in the Nozick-Okin debate), Nozick aims to discuss in his book only the general principles of his view, and refrains from elaborating on more specific spheres, and more specific issues, to which they can be applied.[9] Family justice is not the only specific topic he refrains from

9. "Libertarianism, Feminism, and Relative Identity," 392. I have to disagree, however, with many of Perrett's other claims concerning Okin's argument.

commenting on. He also hardly discusses issues relating to education, old age, environment, nuclear armament, intergenerational justice, multiculturalism, and the fight against racism.

Likewise, Okin writes that "when we have inserted reproductive capacities and work into libertarian equations about ownership . . . we have found that these theories *depend* upon sometimes well hidden and sometimes less well hidden patriarchal assumptions" (110; my emphasis). Notwithstanding the need to fill in some omissions, and to develop libertarian theories further, however, I do not think that Okin has shown that libertarian claims depend on patriarchal or androcentric assumptions.

As before, it is not clear whether Okin's general criticisms of modern political theories in her introduction are meant to apply to Nozick. If they are, however, I believe they are untrue of him. Nozick does not seem to believe that the family is outside the scope of justice. His mention of children and families, and their problematic status within the theory (*Anarchy, State and Utopia,* 38–39, 167–68, 287–91, 330), suggests otherwise. Hence also his failure to sufficiently discuss gender and family justice issues is not likely to be related to a commitment to a public-domestic distinction. Nor does his theory treat women as less than fully human, or assume that only half of the population would be responsible for the domestic sphere.

6

As I mentioned earlier, it is not completely clear whether Okin takes Michael Sandel's *Liberalism and the Limits of Justice* to be pervasively or nonpervasively androcentric. I suggest here that if there are any androcentric omissions in Sandel's theory, they render it only nonpervasively androcentric.

Sandel's book is a general criticism of liberal theories of justice, but he deals mainly with the most important liberal work of the last decades—Rawls's *A Theory of Justice.* One of his objections is directed toward Rawls's claim that "justice is the first virtue of social institutions" (*Theory of Justice,* 3). Okin writes that when Rawls takes justice to be primary, he is not suggesting that it is more elevated than other virtues; justice is primary in the sense that if it is *not* present in a social institution, that institution needs to be reformed or replaced, and cannot be salvaged by the existence of other virtues. Justice is thus to laws and institutions as truth is to theories: an untrue theory should be rejected, even if it has many other benefits. Similarly, a social system that is unjust should be rejected, even if it exhibits many other advantages (Okin, *Justice, Gender and the Family,* 28–29; Rawls, *Theory of Justice,* 3).

Sandel cites Rawls's comparison between truth and theories on the one hand, and justice and social institutions on the other, in order to disagree with it (*Liberalism,* 15). Although he agrees with Rawls that truth is the primary condition of theories, he does not think that justice is the primary condition of social systems. He presents a number of objections, and refers to Rawls's view that justice is necessary because of empirical conditions such as scarcity of resources and people's different purposes and interests (29–30). Rawls believes that, as an empirical matter of fact, such conditions always hold. Therefore, justice is always needed (*Theory of Justice,* 129–30). Sandel disagrees that these empirical conditions *always* hold.[10] He presents as a counterexample some families where—at least at certain times and under some conditions—the empirical conditions Rawls mentions are not present; there is no scarcity of resources, and the purposes, views, and interests of the members of the family by and large coincide. It would seem that justice would not be needed in that context, and hence should not be seen as a primary virtue. Thus, according to Sandel, "justice is the first virtue of social institutions not absolutely, as truth is to theories, but only conditionally, as physical courage is to a war zone" (*Liberalism,* 31). In some situations, such as strife and war, courage is needed. In others, such as peace and tranquility, it is not. Likewise, justice is required in some conditions, but not others, such as a "more or less ideal family situation" (33). Sandel also presents other arguments against Rawls's view, with which one may agree or disagree.

Okin criticizes Sandel for failing to recognize various issues concerning family and gender:

> When we recognize, as we must, that however much the members of families care about one another and share common ends, they are still discrete persons with their own particular aims and hopes, which may sometimes conflict, we must see the family as

---

10. Sandel also claims that even if the empirical generalization were true, it would have not been sufficient to support Rawls's argument. But I will not discuss this issue here.

an institution to which justice is a crucial virtue. When we recognize, as we surely must, that many of the resources that are enjoyed within the sphere of family life—leisure, nurturance, money, time and attention, to name only a few—are by no means always abundant, we see that justice has a highly significant role to play. When we realize that women, especially, are likely to change the whole course of their lives because of their family commitments, it becomes clear that we cannot regard families as analogous to other intimate relations like friendship, however strong the affective bonding of the latter may be. And now that it cannot be assumed . . . that marriage is for life, we must take account of the fact that the decreasing permanence of families renders issues of justice within them more critical than ever. (*Justice, Gender and the Family*, 32)

Okin also takes Sandel to present a romantic, mythic portrayal of the family, as if its participants were close to sainthood, whereas actual families are far more problematic (29–30). I believe, however, that Sandel's discussion shows that he is fully aware that members of families are no saints, that their aims may conflict, that resources are not always abundant, and so forth (*Liberalism,* 31, 33). Nor does he assume that all families are ideal, or are in ideal family situations, although he thinks that *some* families, at *some* times, may be in situations in which justice considerations are unnecessary and it is preferable to guide family behavior by other principles, such as affection or generosity. And his analysis suggests that if the situation changes, it should be possible to resort to justice, although he does not think that the shift from affection and generosity to justice would always be a moral improvement (33). Of course, one may or may not agree with Sandel. Perhaps affection and generosity are not preferable to justice, or they should be accepted only within the limits of what justice would dictate. It does not seem correct, however, to suggest that "in Sandel's view, the family is not characterized by the circumstances of justice, which operate only when interests differ and goods being distributed are scarce" (Okin, *Justice, Gender and the Family,* 26), or to argue against him that "the vision of the family as an institution far above justice pays too little attention to what happens within such groupings when, as is surely common, they fail to meet this saintly ideal" (29). Sandel does not suggest that the family is not characterized by the circumstances of justice, only that some families, when they are in the "more or less ideal family situation" (*Liberalism,* 33), are not character- ized by these circumstances. And he does not seem oblivious to the fact that it is common for families and other groupings to fail to meet this ideal. Okin also seems incorrect in claiming that Sandel's discussion "misapprehends what is meant by the claim that justice is the first or primary virtue of social institutions" (*Justice, Gender and the Family,* 28). According to Okin, Sandel takes the claim that justice is the first or primary virtue to mean that it is the noblest or highest one, thus misun- derstanding Rawls's use of "primary" as "essential." I believe that San- del's discussion, which suggests that some social institutions (for example, the family when it is in the "more or less ideal situation") do not in fact require justice, shows that he fully understands Rawls's use of "primary."

If Okin's general criticisms of contemporary political theories, pre- sented in the introduction to her work, are meant to apply to Sandel's theory, they are untrue of it too. Sandel's discussion of the family shows that he does not take the domestic sphere to be beyond the scope of his theory. Hence, if there are any androcentric omissions (or commissions) in Sandel, they do not seem to be related to a tendency, perhaps influ- enced by the public-domestic dichotomy, to leave the domestic sphere unmentioned, and to take only the public sphere to be within the scope of the theory. Nor does his theory apply to only half of the population, or assume that only half of the population would be responsible for the domestic sphere or treat women as less than fully human.

7

Like Code, Okin should be commended for noting the existence of an- drocentric omissions in philosophy. Her criticisms of MacIntyre, Nozick, and Sandel, however, seem to me exaggerated in a number of ways. First, considering the aim and scope of the works concerned, and the many specific issues that these works could or should have discussed, they should deal with gender justice and family justice issues in less detail than Okin's critique suggests. The works concerned propose to discuss general basic principles rather than specific issues, or to combine a discussion of general principles with that of specific issues. There are also many other issues of importance, including intergenerational justice, education, care of the elderly, environment, business ethics, and biomedical ethics that do not receive full attention. Considering the wide array of subjects some of these works may, or should, deal with, it is unrealistic to expect them to discuss gender justice and family justice issues in detail.

Second, I suggest that Okin's critique also overstates the severity, or grimness, of the androcentricity in the theories she analyzes. The general criticisms of modern political theories (in Okin's introduction to *Justice, Gender and the Family*) are true of *none* of the works she elaborates on.[11] Although there are some omissions in them, the omissions do not justify her far-reaching condemnations. As already noted by Joshua Cohen, Okin hardly mentions gay and lesbian families in her book, and her discussion includes assertions such as "only children who are equally mothered and fathered can develop fully the psychological and moral capacities that currently seem to be unevenly distributed between the sexes" (107).[12] To accept Okin's general criticisms of modern political theories is as justified as accepting, on the basis of her own omissions and commissions, assertions such as that she does not treat lesbians and gay men as full human beings to whom a theory of justice must apply; that a theory whose suggestions for justice in the family do not apply to gay men and lesbians at all will not do; and that her failure to discuss lesbians and gay men is related to some of the other features of her theory. These claims, of course, are overstated, but so are Okin's corresponding claims concerning the political theories she discusses. In a later paper, Okin argues that "rather than being biased *against* homosexual or other non-traditional relationships or families, my arguments taken as a whole are indeed conducive to more, rather than less, acceptance and endorsement of such relationships."[13] She also writes that "there are, admittedly, a few carelessly worded passages in the book that give some credence to the charge of heterosexist bias because they speak of the desirability of children's being reared equally by mothers and fathers. . . . I regret the lack of care taken in such passages, which were meant to apply

---

11. I believe that this is true also of the works of Rawls, Walzer, and Unger that Okin examines, although I do not have the space here to show this in detail. Although there may be some androcentric omissions in these works, almost all of what is written in them is relevant to both sexes and, thus, the theories do not apply to only half of the population (*Justice, Gender and the Family*, 15). They all discuss the family (even if, perhaps, they should have discussed it more), and thus do not consider the domestic sphere outside the scope of social justice (9,15). They nowhere suggest, or imply, that they assume that only women or other specific groups will take care of the domestic issues (15) or that women are not "full human beings to whom a theory of social justice must apply" (23).

12. Cohen, "Okin on Justice, Gender and the Family," 281. See also Okin, *Justice, Gender and the Family*, 100 and 186.

13. "Sexual Orientation and Gender," 44–45; Okin's emphasis.

only in the context of two-parent heterosexual families. However, in the introduction to the book and from time to time throughout I make it clear that I acknowledge the many different forms—two-parent, single-parent, heterosexual, gay and lesbian—that families now take" ("Sexual Orientation and Gender," 57 n. 3). I agree with Okin's argument, but think that the same type of considerations that clear her from charges such as those above should have guided her reading of MacIntyre, Nozick, Sandel, and the other theorists she discusses.

Third, Okin's critique exaggerates the degree of pervasiveness of androcentricity in the theories she discusses. Filling in the omissions, when such exist, is easier than her critique suggests. MacIntyre's, Nozick's and Sandel's theories are, at most, only nonpervasively androcentric.

However, it may be argued that Okin's argument pertains not only to omissions of gender justice and family justice issues in specific *works* in political theory, but also to the *field* of political theory. Okin does not discuss the difference between omissions in works and omissions in fields; however, it is possible for an issue not to be omitted in any specific work in a field, yet to be omitted from the field in general. This can happen when the aims and scopes of all individual works in the field do not require discussion of the issue in question; thus, none of the individual works in the field are in omission for not discussing that issue. However, the field in general is in omission for not discussing that issue, since the issue, being within its scope, should be discussed there.

On the other hand, a certain issue or subject may be omitted in many works within a certain field, yet not be omitted in the field in general. This may happen when the issue is discussed in sufficient elaboration and detail in *other* works in the field. Of course, if all works in the field have omitted the topic, so has the field in general.

Omissions in fields differ from omissions in works also in their temporality. A work is static. An author may correct perceived omissions in it in a later work, but the original work remains as it was. We may read a specific book or article bearing in mind the author's modifications in later works, and we may make our own mental modifications as we read, but the fact remains that these omissions occur in the original work. A field, however, is a dynamic, constantly changing entity that can be corrected and improved over time. Once an omission in a field has been rectified by a treatment of the issue in individual works, the field is no longer guilty of omission, and the omission becomes a matter of historical interest only.

As in works, so in fields, omissions may be pervasive or nonpervasive.

A field, however, is less likely than a work to be pervasively androcentric. This is because we expect different parts of a work to be completely consistent, while we expect a field to include tensions and disagreements.[14] It is easier, therefore, to add an issue to a field than to a work; although some views and theories in the field may conflict with the issue, this would not necessitate rejecting or changing them within the field, and would not make the field pervasively androcentric.

Finally, although the same omission can appear in several works, these works do not "share" the omission, in the sense that if it did not exist in one of them, it would not exist also in others. This is not always so in fields. As a certain topic, subject, or theme may belong to a number of fields and subfields at the same time, so can the omission of that topic or theme. For example, the absence of a certain issue in a discussion of Aquinas may be an omission in philosophy of religion, philosophy of mind, and medieval philosophy. Works that elaborate on this issue in Aquinas can correct the omission in all the fields to which the issue belongs.

How androcentric, then, is political theory, considered as a field? As shown above, some works within political theory have omitted discussion, or sufficient discussion, of issues of gender justice and family justice. On the other hand, some other works, almost all of them written by feminist scholars, have contributed much to the discussion of these topics. In its present state, political theory may still be in omission through not having sufficiently discussed issues of gender justice and family justice, and would thus be androcentric in this respect. But this androcentricity is nonpervasive and can be corrected by additions, which are indeed slowly being introduced. Okin's own work in the final chapter of her book, as well as works by, among others, Jean Bethke Elshtain, Iris Marion Young, Jane Mansbridge, and Anne Phillips, have already raised for discussion and debate many hitherto neglected issues, and thus contributed significantly to reducing the androcentricity by omission in political theory.[15] One can expect that before long, this type of nonpervasive androcentricity will disappear from the field completely.

What has been written here about political philosophy is true also of moral and legal philosophy, philosophy of history, philosophy of social

14. This difference is probably related to, among others, our expectation of a work to be a completed product, while we take most fields to be "works in progress."

15. See, for example, Elshtain, *Power Trips and Other Journeys* and *Women and War*; Young, *Inclusion and Democracy;* Mansbridge, "Feminism and Democratic Community"; and Phillips, *Democracy and Difference.*

sciences, and the history of philosophy. Legal philosophy and moral philosophy, too, have neglected to discuss some issues that are of importance to women. Similarly, the philosophy of history and of the social sciences has overlooked the failure of historians and social scientists to discuss women adequately. As already has been noted by Jean Grimshaw and Okin, in the history of philosophy, too, there is room to comment on explicit androcentric remarks that appear in philosophical systems, and to condemn them.[16] But in all these cases the androcentricity is nonpervasive and can be rectified by various addenda, with no need to reject the fields or works as a whole or to introduce significant changes in them. In some cases, such changes and additions have already been made. Like the type of argument discussed in Chapter 2, the one discussed here shows philosophy to be androcentric only to a limited, nonpervasive extent.

16. Grimshaw, *Philosophy and Feminist Thinking,* 1–2; Okin, *Women in Western Political Thought,* 94–96.

9

A Feminist Alternative?

Some of the arguments I have examined have shown that philosophy is nonpervasively androcentric, that is to say, that it requires some local, limited amendments, additions, or developments. None has shown that philosophy is pervasively androcentric, requiring substantial reform, complete rejection, or replacement by a feminist alternative. Yet some scholars believe that philosophy is pervasively androcentric, and to rectify this predicament they call for, suggest, or point out a nonandrocentric philosophy to replace what they take to be the present pervasively androcentric one.

While nonpervasive androcentricity calls for nonpervasive changes, pervasive androcentricity calls for a pervasive revolution, which would go beyond merely developing or adding to existing discourse. Such a revolution is frequently described as suggesting an alternative to all or most existing philosophy by presenting new methodological principles or fundamental presuppositions. Thus Laura Lyn Inglis and Peter K. Steinfeld, for example, write that "feminist philosophy must become self-conscious in the appropriation of patriarchal texts. To do so requires a way, a path, a hermeneutical method. We propose that this hermeneutical method be informed by and infused with subversion, a subversion that can transform the whole of the past."[1] They also talk of this method as providing "a model of the rethinking of the entire Western heritage" (6). According to Alison Jaggar, "One of the main contributions of radical feminism has

1. *Old Dead White Men's Philosophy*, xiv.

been its demonstration that the prevailing culture is suffused with the perceptions and values of male dominance. In response to this recognition, radical feminists have made it one of their political priorities to create an alternative women's culture."[2] Carole Pateman writes that "to develop a theory in which women and femininity have an autonomous place means that the private and the public, the social and the political, also have to be *completely* reconceptualized; in short, it means *an end* to a long history of sexually particular theory that masquerades as universalism. Whether or not patriarchal theory is ultimately subverted, this book, along with other recent feminist theory, shows that a very rich and exciting beginning has been made."[3] And Beverly Thiele calls for a new, gynocentric political philosophy that "not only challenges and transforms the *content* of political philosophy; it also challenges and transforms its *methodology*. In taking off from our critique of male-stream thought we are sensitized to the political uses of the male-stream's magic tricks and do not have to perform on the same terms. . . . We are not only looking at a different subject: we are also doing a different type of scholarship."[4] Catharine MacKinnon, too, argues that

> women's experience of politics, of life as sex object, gives rise to its own method of appropriating that reality: feminist method. As *its own kind* of social analysis, within yet outside the male paradigm just as women's lives are, it has a *distinctive* theory of the *relation* between method and truth, the individual and her social surroundings, the presence and place of the natural and spiritual in culture and society, and social being and causality itself.[5]

Such scholars, then, would not accept Martha Nussbaum's view that

> to do feminist philosophy is simply to get on with the tough work of theorizing in a rigorous and throughgoing way, but

2. *Feminist Politics and Human Nature*, 382. Note that not all the authors mentioned here discuss philosophy specifically; some discuss knowledge or culture in general (which, of course, includes philosophy).

3. "Introduction," 9–10; my emphases. Okin cites the first of these sentences (approvingly, it seems) in *Women in Western Political Thought*, 315.

4. "Vanishing Acts," 41–43; Thiele's emphases.

5. "Feminism, Marxism, Method and the State: An Agenda for Theory," 535–36; the first two emphases are mine. For some further examples, see Cixous, "Laugh of the Medusa," 245; Flax, "Political Philosophy," 270; Gross, "Conclusion," 195–96; Held, *Feminist Morality*, 43; Narayan, "Project of Feminist Epistemology," 256; Schott, "Resurrecting Embodiment," 171; and some of the claims cited in Chapter 1.

without the blind spots, the ignorance of fact, and the moral obtuseness that have characterized much philosophical thought about women and sex and the family and ethics in the male-dominated academy.[6]

For them, more is needed: an entire, pervasive revolution, affecting the methodological presuppositions or fundamental principles of philosophy.[7] Such hopes or agendas are only to be expected. If philosophy is pervasively androcentric, an entire philosophical or intellectual revolution, which would go far beyond Nussbaum's suggestion, is indeed necessary. If "new wine must not be poured into old bottles," as Maria Mies declares in the epigraph to one of her papers, and if "the master's tools will never dismantle the master's house," as Audre Lorde titles one of hers, then new bottles or new tools must indeed be found.[8] This chapter argues that such radical alternatives to existing philosophy have not been found, and that this fact joins the critiques presented in previous chapters in indicating that the view concerning the pervasive androcentricity of philosophy is problematic.

2

Examining the way almost all feminist philosophers actually philosophize does not reveal any unique methodology. When one reads feminist philosophers, one encounters by and large the methodologies and basic principles found in nonfeminist philosophy. Feminist philosophers, too, present evidence; point out relevant facts; note their sources; explain; analyze information; draw distinctions; note contradictions, inconsistencies, and inaccuracies in others' arguments; or (in the case of postmodernist feminists) describe and deconstruct in a postmodernist manner. They too employ hierarchies, dichotomies, and different degrees of essentialism and claim a degree of nonsubjective status for their claims. There are, of course, differences in content. Many feminist texts discuss and develop issues that nonfeminist texts have neglected and correct mistakes

---

6. "Feminists and Philosophy," 63.

7. For simplicity's sake, I will frequently refer in this chapter to methodological presuppositions or fundamental principles as "methodology."

8. Mies, "Towards a Methodology," 117; Lorde, "The Master's Tools," 110. Lorde is clearly incorrect at least on the literal level of this assertion: one can in fact dismantle one's master's house with the master's tools.

that some nonfeminist texts have made. This philosophical contribution is important and helpful, but it does not amount to employing different methodologies of the type that the scholars mentioned in the previous section aim at and call for. Similarly, feminist hierarchical dichotomies (for example, oppression of women is a worse condition than their liberation), generalizations (for example, women are oppressed), or essentialist claims (for example, women are not inferior to men) discuss issues that appear only infrequently in hierarchical dichotomies, generalizations, or essentialist claims in other philosophical spheres. But the fundamental principles and methods employed are similar. Occasionally one also finds differences in style; but differences in style hardly amount to differences in methodology, or alternatives to basic principles, of the type called for by the authors I have cited. Feminist texts can be understood by any intelligent person, feminist or nonfeminist, woman or man, irrespective of orientation, and there is nothing in the texts to testify that feminist philosophizing differs in methodology from nonfeminist. If one were exposed only to the methodological aspects of feminist works, without knowing their contents or programmatic backgrounds, one could not infer that they are employed in feminist rather than other contexts.

It may be answered that although *actual* feminist philosophizing does not reveal a new or unique methodology, various descriptions of or prescriptions for the new methodology (not all of which were initially proposed in the context of the present discussion) do present distinct alternatives. However, some of these suggestions follow earlier nonfeminist alternatives that have already been typical of large parts of mainstream philosophy. Perhaps the most famous effort to present such a new feminist methodology is related to Carol Gilligan's discussion of care ethics. But as has been shown in Chapter 7, significant parts of Western ethics already have the characteristics attributed to care ethics, and other ethical teachings present admixtures of justice characteristics and care characteristics.

Alessandra Tanesini, too, argues for a methodological innovation related to work on sexual harassment:

> Once feminist politics has unearthed the true significance of the offensive remark, the epistemic relevance of referring to one's feeling to justify the claim that the "joke" was offensive can be recognized. The harasser might not be willing to listen, but it is now possible to recast this unwillingness as self-serving irrationality. Feminist political interventions on this topic have *changed*

the standards of reasoning by giving epistemic legitimacy to claims that could not otherwise be justified.[9]

However, there already were several legal precedents where feelings corroborated claims for offensiveness, before sexual harassment legislation was suggested. Examples include cases of libel and slander, invasion of privacy, threats, and racial or ethnic slurs. Nor is the notion that feelings are important in moral considerations new. Either way, the claim that the work on sexual harassment has changed the standards of reasoning seems overstated.

Some other descriptions of or suggestions for a new methodology follow previous nonfeminist alternatives that have been less typical, or atypical, of mainstream philosophy. However, they are in discord with most actual feminist work. This is the case, for example, with some portrayals of feminist thought and methodology, suggested by some radical feminists and presented (critically) by Alison Jaggar.[10] Jaggar describes, for example, discussions of the feminist or feminine cognitive-intuitive power, which is supposed to endow its practitioners with unmediated knowledge of others' feelings or motives. Another cognitive capacity is the mystical-spiritual ability to connect with other people or with nature as a whole. Susan Griffin, for example, takes women to identify with nature around them to the extent that the subject-object relationship is significantly blurred, so that inspection of nature is, in a way, nature's inspection of itself.[11] Mary Daly, too, seeing the world as an organic whole, rejects dichotomies, separations, and distinctions.[12] Jaggar also describes other feminist scholars who emphasize the inseparability of the knower from the known, or rely on feelings rather than reasoning, or refuse the "false clarity" of "androcentric" thinking from yet other directions (*Feminist Politics and Human Nature,* 368).[13]

Other portrayals of a new methodology that are atypical of previous mainstream philosophy emphasize consciousness raising.[14] Catharine

---

9. *Introduction to Feminist Epistemologies,* 228; my emphasis.

10. See Jaggar, *Feminist Politics and Human Nature,* 364–69.

11. *Woman and Nature,* 226; cited in Jaggar, *Feminist Politics and Human Nature,* 366.

12. *Beyond God the Father,* 42–43; cited in Jaggar, *Feminist Politics and Human Nature,* 367.

13. Many of the characteristics of Griffin's, Daly's, and the other alternatives critically discussed by Jaggar already appear in mainstream, nonfeminist, para-psychological, mystical, Romantic, and Heideggerian thought. But I will not pursue this line of discussion here.

14. Consciousness-raising of various types has been employed also in socialist, utopian,

MacKinnon, for example, claims that "Consciousness raising is the major technique of analysis, structure of organization, method of practice, and theory of social change of the women's movement."[15] Similarly, Nancy Hartsock argues that

> when we look at the contemporary feminist movement in all its variety, we find that while many of the questions we addressed were not new, there is a methodology common among feminists that differs from the practice of most social movements, particularly from those in advanced capitalist countries. At bottom, feminism is a mode of analysis, a method of approaching life and politics, rather than a set of political conclusions about the oppression of women.
>
> The practice of small-group consciousness raising, with its stress on examining and understanding experience and on connecting personal experience to the structures that define our lives, is the clearest example of the method basic to feminism.[16]

However, as Sandra Harding argues, "We can ask what the point would be of elaborating a theory of the distinctive nature of feminist inquiry that excluded the best feminist social science research from satisfying its criteria."[17] Harding makes this point concerning feminist discussions in the social sciences, but the problem is pertinent, of course, for other fields as well: suggestions such as those above are in discord with most actual feminist work, and their characteristics clash with the characteristics of the methodologies that almost all feminist philosophers actually use. Almost no feminist scholarship and philosophizing connects directly with the world as a whole, blurs the subject-object distinction, or follows the mode of consciousness raising; most rather present arguments, show evidence, and reply to objections.

The discord between such methodologies and most actual feminist work is problematic. If the suggested methodologies are needed as alternatives to (what is taken to be) pervasive androcentric philosophizing,

---

and religious groups, as well as in support groups and some group therapies. Perhaps the most famous antecedent to feminist consciousness-raising has been "conscientization" in radical education and liberation theology. See, for example, Freire, *Pedagogy of the Oppressed,* esp. chap. 3.

15. "Feminism, Marxism, Method and the State: An Agenda for Theory," 519.
16. "Fundamental Feminism," 35.
17. "Introduction," 5.

then failing to follow them makes philosophizing androcentric. But this would indicate that most feminist thought is androcentric. And if it is important to reject androcentricity, then most feminist philosophizing should be rejected as well. If, on the other hand, one wants to continue to rely on most feminist thought, as well as to see it as feminist, then the methodological characteristics of most "mainstream" philosophical thought should also not be seen as androcentric. They allow androcentric, nonandrocentric, and feminist discussions and agendas, and there is no need to reject or replace them with feminist alternative methodologies. The importance of, or the need for, the suggested nonandrocentric alternatives thus becomes doubtful.

Some suggestions for an alternative methodology seem to be prescriptions of what should be employed in the future rather than descriptions of what is used in the present. Thus Hélène Cixous, for example, envisages her alternative *l'écriture féminine,* a feminine style of writing, as a mode of writing or philosophizing that is yet to be achieved.[18] However, the problems identified above are as valid when the suggested methodologies are seen as prescriptive rather than descriptive. Again, if these would-be methodologies are needed as alternatives to androcentric philosophizing, and failing to follow them makes philosophizing androcentric, then most feminist thought, about almost any subject, is androcentric, and as such should be rejected. And if one feels one can continue to rely on and employ most actual feminist work, then once again one does not need to reject most of the methodological characteristics of Western philosophy, nor is it necessary to suggest alternatives to them.

3

Other descriptions of or prescriptions for alternative methodologies combine the problems I have outlined—similarity to significant parts of nonfeminist research, and exclusion of significant parts of feminist research—with a discussion of issues of *content* rather than of methodology. Scholars who present such accounts emphasize that their methodologies deal with women's issues, point out women's concerns, focus on feminist views, and so on. However, these are examples of employing old methodologies or fundamental structures to deal with feminist issues by

18. However, Cixous is somewhat unclear on this issue, since she also states that *l'écriture féminine* already exists. See "Laugh of the Medusa," 245, 253.

"adding" women to them (which is just what the authors cited at the beginning of this chapter wanted to avoid), and again suggests that many of the methodologies and basic assumptions in philosophy are not andro-centric, since they can be employed to discuss antifeminist, nonfeminist, and feminist issues. The commitment to *feminist* issues and agendas (rather than, say, to religious, scientific, or ontological issues and agendas) has little to do with innovation in the methodology, which could just as well be applied to other fields or ideologies. Rhoda Linton, for example, points out that the characteristics she identifies are of "both process and content," and does not seem to share the purposes of the authors cited in section 1. She ascribes the following list of characteristics to feminist methodologies:

1. Women are the *active* central focus/subject.
2. Cooperative group activity is the predominant modus operandi.
3. There is a recognized need for liberation from the oppression of the status quo.
4. Issues affecting women are identified, and strategies for action are developed.
5. There is an open, inclusive, accessible, creative, dynamic process between people, among activities, or in relation to ideas.
6. There is a commitment to respect and include women's ideas, theories, experiences, and action strategies from diverse experiences that appear to be, and sometimes are, in conflict.[19]

Characteristics 1, 3, the first part of 4, and part of 6 concern the subject matter, agendas, and political or social aims of the methodologies.[20] Characteristic 2 is untrue of most feminist philosophical texts, which are authored by single scholars. Cooperative group activity is more typical, rather, of the exact sciences, which are frequently portrayed in feminist thinking as the antithesis of feminist scholarship. It may be answered that "cooperative group activity" is meant here in its moderate sense, more common in the humanities, namely, as merely involving discussion of one's work with colleagues and friends, receiving comments on earlier drafts, and so on. But if this is what is meant, the characteristic is equally true of nonfeminist philosophy. The second part of characteristic 4, that

19. "Toward a Feminist Research Method," 276; Linton's emphasis.
20. By "subject" in (1) Linton may be referring to the researchers rather than the re-searched. But this too is a characteristic not of the methodology itself, but only of those practicing it.

"strategies for action are developed," is untrue of the greater part of feminist philosophizing; very few feminist philosophical works involve actual strategies of action. Again, it may be replied that this characteristic is understood in a more moderate sense. If so, it would be true of some feminist work, since some feminist arguments do *imply* some general courses of action. But then this characteristic would be true also of many general philosophical theses and arguments, especially in epistemology, moral philosophy, and political theory. Similarly, characteristic 5, that "there is an open, inclusive, accessible, creative, dynamic process between people, among activities, or in relation to ideas," is not more true of many feminist philosophical works than of many general ones. I believe that characteristic 6, concerning the "commitment to respect and include . . . ideas, theories, experiences, and action strategies from diverse experiences," is also not realized in feminist works more than in nonfeminist ones. Feminist texts are not extraordinarily inclusive of diverse perspectives, and like nonfeminist texts include mainly their authors' arguments, views, and perspectives, while those of other people are presented either in order to credit first authorship or to be argued against. Nor are feminist philosophical works more respectful or inclusive of others' views than are general philosophical works. They tend to be respectful of what is considered within the feminist tradition, but are not extraordinarily so of what is considered outside it.[21] The latter part of characteristic 6, that ideas, theories, experiences, and so on, will be respected even if they are or appear to be in conflict, is again not more true of feminist philosophical works than of general ones. When the ideas, theories, experiences, and so on are nonfeminist, or appear to be in conflict with feminist experiences, theories, or ideas, they are not extraordinarily respected.

4

Other, more moderate proposals would be stronger, but remain problematic. Such proposals would consciously identify with a certain existing philosophical tradition and take only the other parts of Western philoso-

21. Some of the feminist works discussed in previous chapters can serve as examples. See also discussions of nonfeminist women's views in Jaggar, *Feminist Politics and Human Nature*, 149–51; Flax, "Political Philosophy," 270; and Frye, *Politics of Reality*, 60. See also the authors critically discussed in Davis, "Remaking the She-Devil," esp. 21–23, 34, 40.

phy to be pervasively androcentric. For example, it might be suggested that only non-postmodernist philosophy is pervasively androcentric, while postmodernist philosophy is only nonpervasively androcentric, or even not androcentric at all. In such a case, feminist arguments for the pervasive androcentricity of philosophy need not present an alternative to all Western philosophy, but can employ (with minor or no alterations) some part of it, while rejecting as pervasively androcentric all the rest.

Such proposals are stronger in one respect than many of those considered earlier, since they do not aim, and thus are not open to the criticism that they have failed, to present an alternative to the whole of philosophy. However, they too would characterize most of feminist philosophizing (in the example above, all non-postmodernist feminist philosophical work) as pervasively androcentric, and hence are plausible only for those feminists who are ready to give up, or reject as androcentric, all work except that done within their own "school." Those postmodernist feminists who would wish to continue to employ also other types of feminist thought (that is, non-postmodernist feminist thought) would again thereby imply that the methodologies of these other types, as well as of the parallel types of general, nonfeminist thought, are not pervasively androcentric. These methodologies would emerge, again, as amenable to feminist, antifeminist, and nonfeminist usage, and whose problematic use is related to content rather than method. Thus it would become unclear, once again, why one needs radically different methodological alternatives. Although I am sure that feminist postmodernists willing to reject the whole of feminist philosophy except their own (or followers of other feminist methodologies who are willing to completely reject the whole of feminist philosophy except their own) do exist, their number, I suspect, is small.

5

The trend of feminist philosophy under discussion here thus has put itself in a difficult position. Having made very broad (and as I have attempted to show in this book, unjustified) claims about the pervasive androcentricity of Western philosophy, it called for an alternative that it could not realize and anticipated a revolution it could not implement. Feminist philosophy is methodologically similar to the rest of the philosophical tradition. If the philosophical tradition should be rejected as pervasively androcentric on methodological grounds, so should most of feminist philosophy. On the other hand, if feminist philosophy is perceived not to be pervasively androcentric on methodological grounds, so should be most of the philosophical tradition.

This, of course, is not the first time in the history of philosophy that a methodological revolution has been suggested, and other schools of thought renounced. However, the trend in feminist philosophy discussed here has radicalized and combined various characteristics of this effort in a particularly problematic way. First, it has presented as androcentric a large number of general presuppositions or methodological principles, thus ruling out their use in feminist theory itself. The more inclusive the rejection, the less the theory itself has to work with. On the other hand, the more methodological assumptions are deemed legitimate, the more of them the theory itself can employ, but then also the less radical and inclusive the theory's criticisms of other theories' use of these methodological principles must be. It is difficult to think of many revolutionary methodological movements in philosophy that have castigated so large a number of such basic and general presuppositions or methodological principles (for example, concerning distinctions, regularities, hierarchies, essentialism, and general logical presuppositions) as has this trend. Cartesianism and logical positivism, for example, did not reject as many methodological assumptions. They presented one or several new methodological principles as an addition to the many preceding ones, distinguishing themselves from and rejecting previous methodologies and philosophies that lacked this addition. Sometimes the added methodological components altered, or even canceled, some of the previous ones; but many methodological components remained untouched, or only slightly modified. Such, for example, are the rules of formal and informal logic, the use of distinctions, hierarchies, generalizations, and so on. Postmodernism and Kierkegaardian and Nietzschean existentialism are some of the very few examples of intellectual methodological revolutions that have rejected as much as the feminist trend discussesd here has. Not surprisingly, they too are quite limited in what can be done with them philosophically. There are many moral, spiritual, political, interpersonal, or casual everyday decisions and challenges that one cannot cope with when one excludes so many other methodologies, confining oneself to postmodernist or existentialist methodologies alone.

Second, unlike logical positivism, postmodernism, Cartesianism, and some other schools of thought, the trend in question here has not, in fact, suggested any new methodological principles to which it could adhere while rejecting so many of the others. If it had succeeded in introducing a satisfactory methodological revolution, which it could present as an alternative to what it has so broadly condemned, the condemnation would seem, in this respect, more acceptable. The contribution of feminist philosophy, however, has not had to do with issues of a new methodology.

Finally, more than Cartesianism, postmodernism, and so forth, feminist philosophy is variegated, having been influenced by a very wide spectrum of theories. It is thus more difficult for a feminist theorist of the trend critiqued here to discard various methodological principles without also discarding many parts of feminist theory.

The claim that philosophy is pervasively androcentric, then, involves theorists making the assertion in too many difficulties, even according to what are frequently their own criteria and assumptions, and for this reason, too, the claim is best rejected. Of course, it may be replied that feminist philosophy is still very young. A distinctive feminist alternative may still emerge. I believe this is true, as is the fact that whatever we say about feminism, whether critical or complimentary, is only tentative and may yet change. This should not prevent us, however, from discussing the characteristics of the field as it currently is. It seems to me unlikely that a distinctive philosophical alternative will emerge that would satisfy the criteria posed by the scholars mentioned above, but of course I may be proven wrong. At present, we can only examine feminist philosophy as it is, without overlooking the significance of the lack of an alternative, distinctive feminist methodology.

10

Concluding Remarks

I

This book has argued that philosophy is androcentric, but significantly less so than frequently claimed. Philosophy is not in any way pervasively androcentric, and in most ways it is not even nonpervasively androcentric. Three types of arguments—that from explicit androcentric views, that from androcentric metaphors, and that from androcentric omissions—show it to be nonpervasively androcentric, and no argument successfully shows it to be pervasively androcentric. Moreover, some of the arguments that show philosophy to be nonpervasively androcentric present it as more androcentric than it really is. Attempts that have been made to liberate philosophy from its presumed pervasive androcentricity by presenting radically different alternatives have been neither necessary nor successful. Philosophy emerges, in almost all of its parts, as human rather than male, and most parts and aspects of it need not be rejected or rewritten.

Various general objections may be raised, however, against these claims. One such objection is that philosophy has not been revealed as more androcentric since it, or our entire culture, is so saturated with androcentricity that we cannot notice it any more. According to this proposition, since everything is androcentric, androcentricity cannot be distinguished and identified, just as if everything were blue we would not be able to notice blueness and thus blueness would be meaningless to us. However, we frequently do distinguish between what is androcentric and what is not, and do identify cases of androcentricity and understand what the notion means. Thus, for example, we take Schopenhauer's assertions regarding women to be androcentric, and many parts of feminist philosophy to be nonandrocentric. Moreover, if it were true that we cannot notice androcentricity, and that it has no meaning for us, there would be no reason to be bothered by it or to try to correct and change it in any way. Note also that the totalizing claim that everything is androcentric (although we cannot notice it) is as strong as the claim that—although we cannot notice it—everything is in fact gynocentric, or just, or loving.

Another possible objection is that the discussion in this book isolates from one another the various types of arguments for the androcentricity of philosophy. Each type is examined on its own, shown to be flawed, and then rejected or qualified. However, it may be argued, if the arguments were considered together, the claim for the pervasive androcentricity of philosophy would be proven. For example, Genevieve Lloyd employs arguments from explicit androcentric statements as well as arguments from associations and stereotypes. I discuss her use of the latter type of arguments in Chapter 3; other authors' arguments from explicit androcentric statements are considered separately in Chapter 2, but since Lloyd does not use this type of argument as elaborately as do some other authors, she is not mentioned there. Similarly, MacKinnon's arguments concerning objectivity and objectification are considered in Chapter 4, while her arguments concerning metaphors are considered separately, in Chapter 5. It might be objected that if all of MacKinnon's arguments were considered together, the pervasive androcentricity of philosophy would be proven. This might also be maintained regarding other scholars who employ more than one type of argument, and even regarding arguments used by different scholars.

However, considering the arguments for the androcentricity of philosophy together would not prove the pervasive androcentricity of philosophy, since the objections to each argument are not invalidated, or responded to, by the other arguments. The arguments do not compensate for each other's weaknesses. Hence, treating them together would not have shown that philosophy is pervasively androcentric.

Another objection might claim that the critiques offered in this book are circular. They employ rational, philosophical methodologies, themselves allegedly androcentric, to determine whether Western philosophy is androcentric. By applying such methodologies, it may be objected, the critiques already assume the conclusion, namely, that philosophy is not androcentric. By using philosophical, rational methods, the outcome of the discussion is determined from the outset.

However, the application of philosophical, rational methodologies does not in itself assume that philosophy and rationality will be defended and found nonandrocentric. Rational and philosophical methodologies have frequently been used to criticize philosophy and rationality, and have sometimes led to the conclusion that philosophy, or rationality, or parts and aspects of them, should be abandoned or reformed. From skepticism and relativism to Gödel's Theorem and "Grue," philosophy and rational thought have shown that they have the resources, and can be used, to criticize and reform many of their own characteristics and presuppositions. Moreover, in this book philosophy *has* been found, through the use of philosophical and rational methods, to be androcentric in certain ways, and in principle could have been found to be so also in all other ways. The use of philosophical-rational considerations, then, does not presuppose that philosophy is nonandrocentric, and thus is not circular.

It may be suggested that the circularity of the argumentation becomes apparent if it is portrayed not as inquiring whether or not philosophy is *androcentric*, but whether or not philosophy is *acceptable*. In employing philosophy or reason, it might be argued, one is assuming that they are acceptable, thus determining what the conclusion will be by already including it in the premises. However, in employing philosophy and reason one is assuming only that these are *initially* acceptable. As the foregoing examples demonstrate, it is possible for reason and philosophy, after making this temporary assumption, to reach the conclusion that, because of certain problems, they need to be partly or radically altered or even rejected.

Moreover, the arguments for the androcentricity of philosophy—except, perhaps, the postmodernist ones—try to convince readers by using rational criteria. As shown in the preceding chapter, they too draw distinctions, present facts, and use other forms of conventional argumentation. Thus, they presuppose that rational argumentation is a legitimate tool for examining whether philosophy is androcentric, and for showing that it is. Examining whether these rational arguments prove what they profess to prove by employing nonrational criteria would have been unhelpful. It would also treat feminist philosophy as if it were unserious. The critiques presented in this book, then, follow the methodological assumptions supposed in the arguments critiqued.

This relates to another possible objection. It may be argued that the critiques I present are ineffectual since they are irrelevant for those theorists who employ *non*rational procedures in judging philosophy to be androcentric. For such theorists, it may be argued, none of the critiques offered in this study is pertinent.

This objection is justified; for such philosophers, none of the critiques is pertinent. My arguments are indeed not intended for those who reject the use of rational criteria; they are intended for another, wider, audience. We can consider groups of people for whom the critiques presented in this book would be relevant. First, the arguments would be relevant for all those theorists who reach their conclusions about the androcentricity of philosophy by using rational methods. This group includes almost all the feminist authors discussed in this book and those who are convinced by their arguments, since almost all of them employ rational arguments to show that philosophy is androcentric. The argumentation presented here is pertinent also for the great majority of feminists who write about any subject in any field, since almost all of them use rational criteria, and hence the arguments and critiques presented in this book are as relevant for them as those they themselves use.

The critiques presented in this study are relevant also for those who are sympathetic to feminism, but are uncertain with which of its theses they agree, and who employ rational considerations when they think about these issues. The arguments in this book are relevant also for those who do not subscribe to feminism or are sympathetic to it but want to learn more about it, and who employ rational considerations. And the discussion may even be useful for those—feminist and nonfeminist alike—who are not sure whether they do or do not want to employ rational criteria. Such readers will find here examples of how the question of the androcentricity of philosophy can be addressed rationally. This may help them to decide whether they want to consider the question in a rational way, or to form an opinion by some other means.

Surely these are the majority of the likely readers of this work. However, no work can be useful to everyone, and for some—the small group of those who reject altogether the use of reason—the book is, indeed, irrelevant. They might instead use, for example, an unexplicated intuition that philosophy is androcentric. Or they may entertain a vague and complex postmodernist discourse that concludes with the statement that philosophy is androcentric. Or they may rely on jokes and whimsicalities that suggest the androcentricity of philosophy. However, just as the considerations presented in this book are not pertinent for those who do not judge by rational criteria, the considerations of this latter group are not relevant for those who judge by reason. Those who do want to determine by reason whether, or to what extent, philosophy is androcentric need not pay any heed to conclusions arrived at by unexplicated intuition, foggy deconstruction, or mere caprice.

2

Considering the arguments for the androcentricity of philosophy together enables us to observe two problems common to some of them.
One is the tendency to exaggerate, generalize, and relate to certain phenomena or facts disproportionately. True, many of these facts or phenomena often have not been sufficiently noticed, and it is important to
point them out. However, this is sometimes accompanied by an exaggera-
tion of the relative significance of these facts or phenomena, and by an
insufficient regard for other, pertinent ones. By incorrect induction or
extrapolation, what was hitherto unnoticed, and is true of some components, is sometimes pronounced true of most or all. This methodological
error can be seen, for example, when certain metaphors (Chapter 5) and
certain androcentric statements (Chapter 2) are taken to implicate entire
philosophies, when certain omissions are taken to entirely tarnish certain
systems (Chapter 8), or when certain harmful applications of notions
(such as objectivity, or abstraction) are taken to disqualify all their uses
(Chapter 4). Of course, the androcentric elements that exist in philosophical theories should not be ignored or concealed. But one should take
care not to try to correct one unbalanced portrayal of philosophical theories by presenting another.

A second problem relates to the tendency to present women and men
as very different, or complete opposites, ignoring all that they share. It
seems to be forgotten that women are not only women, and men are not
only men; they are also human beings, and as such share many interests,
values, and characteristics. This tendency is evident in the almost complete neglect of the similarities between women and men in many of the
arguments concerning interests and values (Chapter 6) and concerning
mentalities (Chapter 7). It can also be seen in many of the arguments
considered in Chapter 8, where general discussions of people's rights,
property, utility, justice, and so on, are presumed not to apply to women.

It is important to restate, however, some cautionary remarks made in
the introduction, and to correct possible misunderstandings. Showing
that philosophy is less androcentric than frequently claimed does not
show that there is something wrong with the feminist project itself; one
can be a feminist, yet reject various (or even all) arguments for the androcentricity of philosophy. The general goals of feminism, as well as almost
all of its specific objectives, are not affected by the question of the androcentricity of philosophy. Likewise, the argument that philosophy is less
androcentric than frequently claimed should not be seen as an attack on

feminist philosophy. Like almost all other philosophical fields, feminist philosophy, too, is highly varied, and includes many disagreements and debates. The androcentricity question is one of them. It should be remembered that there are many feminist philosophers who accept the views or arguments critiqued here, many who do not, and many who do not deal with this question at all, working on others. Generalizing from problems with some arguments presented in some feminist works to the whole of feminist philosophy and theory is as problematic as generalizing from some androcentric elements in some nonfeminist works to philosophical theories at large, or to Western philosophy at large, condemning the whole of it as pervasively androcentric.

3

The discussion in this book sought to examine whether various claims concerning the androcentricity of philosophy are true, and presupposed that they should be accepted or rejected on this basis alone. However, some believe that philosophical discourse should accept conclusions wholly or partly based on the extent of their helpfulness to women. I find this view highly problematic on a number of counts, but will not pursue this matter here. Let us grant, however, for the sake of discussion, that helpfulness to women is relevant to accepting or rejecting conclusions in a philosophical inquiry. Are the conclusions reached in this book helpful to women?

The answer to this question, I believe, is completely contingent on the truth of the conclusions: if the conclusions are true, they are helpful to women, and if they are untrue, they are unhelpful. If they are true, they distinguish correctly between what is androcentric in philosophy and what is not, leaving those parts of philosophy that are not harmful to women untouched, and pointing out only those that are harmful. If the conclusions reached in this book are untrue because philosophy is in fact more androcentric than suggested here, then they are unhelpful to women, since they call for rejecting fewer themes and issues than need to be rejected. If the conclusions are untrue because philosophy is in fact less androcentric than suggested here, then again they are unhelpful since they call for rejecting and replacing more themes and issues than actually need to be rejected and replaced.

It may be also asked whether the conclusions reached here are helpful to feminist research. The answer, I believe, is similar to the one given to the previous question. Feminist research can be considered as a truth-seeking enterprise, or as a political endeavor. I have many difficulties with the latter suggestion, but will consider them both. As a truth-seeking enterprise, feminist research seeks to reach true conclusions about its subject matter. If the conclusions of this book are true, they help feminist research realize this purpose, and thus are helpful to it. If feminist research is not considered a truth-seeking enterprise, but, rather, a political endeavor, its objective is surely to help women. If, as argued above, true conclusions concerning the androcentricity of philosophy are helpful to women, then adopting them would further this political end.

Moreover, although feminist philosophy deals with a variety of issues and concerns, significant segments of it have been preoccupied with the effort to identify the pervasively androcentric character of philosophy and to find alternatives to it, and much work and energy have been dedicated to these ends. If the conclusions of this book are true, these efforts should be abandoned. This may clear space for other concerns, and allow the devotion of much scholarly work to other theoretical and practical ends. A deep cultural and philosophical revolution, or the creation of a counterculture, can be great achievements and of much help, if they are needed. But if they are not needed, they can also turn into a great—and unnecessary—burden, and involve much waste of time and energy.

Many philosophers still seem to believe that significantly reforming, rejecting, or replacing large sections of philosophy with a feminist alternative will improve philosophy and help women. If the critiques presented in this book are correct, however, the *loci* for developing philosophy, and for being of service to women, lie elsewhere.

Bibliography

Agassi, Joseph. "The Lark and the Tortoise." *Philosophy of the Social Sciences* 19 (1989): 89–94.

Antony, Louise M. "Is Psychological Individualism a Piece of Ideology?" *Hypatia* 10 (1995): 157–74.

Atherton, Margaret. "Cartesian Reason and Gendered Reason." In *A Mind of One's Own: Feminist Essays on Reason and Objectivity,* ed. Louise M. Antony and Charlotte Witt, 19–34. Boulder, Colo.: Westview Press, 1993.

Baier, Annette C. "Hume: The Reflective Women's Epistemologist?" In *Moral Prejudices: Essays on Ethics,* 76–94. Cambridge: Harvard University Press, 1994.

———. "Hume, The Women's Moral Theorist?" In *Moral Prejudices: Essays on Ethics,* 51–75. Cambridge: Harvard University Press, 1994.

———. "Rhyme and Reason: Reflections on Davidson's Version of Having Reasons." In *Actions and Events: Perspectives on the Philosophy of Donald Davidson,* ed. Ernest LePore and Brian P. McLaughlin, 116–129. Oxford: Blackwell, 1985.

Bataille, George. *Death and Sexuality.* New York: Arno, 1977.

Beauvoir, Simone de. *The Second Sex.* Harmondsworth: Penguin, 1972.

Black, Max. "Metaphor." In *Models and Metaphors: Studies in Language and Philosophy,* 25–47. Ithaca: Cornell University Press, 1962.

———. "More About Metaphor." In *Metaphor and Thought,* ed. Andrew Ortony, 19–43. Cambridge: Cambridge University Press, 1979.

Braidotti, Rosi. *Patterns of Dissonance: A Study of Women in Contemporary Philosophy.* Translated by Elizabeth Guild. Cambridge: Polity Press, 1991.

Buber, Martin. *I and Thou.* Translated by Walter Kaufmann. New York: Charles Scribner's Sons, 1970.

Camus, Albert. *The Plague.* Translated by Stuart Gilbert. London: Hutchinson, 1967.

Cixous, Hélène. "The Laugh of the Medusa." In *New French Feminisms,* edited by Elaine Marks and Isabelle de Courtivron, translated by Keith Cohen and Paula Cohen, 245–64. Brighton: Harvester, 1981.

———. "Sorties." In Hélène Cixous and Catherine Clément, *The Newly Born Woman,* trans. Betsy Wing, 63–132. Minneapolis: University of Minnesota Press, 1986.

Code, Lorraine. *What Can She Know? Feminist Theory and the Construction of Knowledge.* Ithaca: Cornell University Press, 1991.

Cohen, Joshua. "Okin on Justice, Gender and the Family." *Canadian Journal of Philosophy* 22 (1992): 263–86.

Collins, Patricia Hill. "The Social Construction of Black Feminist Thought." In *Women, Knowledge and Reality: Explorations in Feminist Philosophy,* 2nd ed., ed. Ann Garry and Marilyn Pearsall, 222–48. New York: Routledge, 1996.

Crick, Nicki R., and Jennifer K. Grotepeter. "Relational Aggression, Gender, and Social Psychological Adjustment." *Child Development* 66 (1995): 710–22.

Daly, Mary. *Beyond God the Father: Toward a Philosophy of Women's Liberation.* Boston: Beacon, 1973.

Davidson, Donald. "Paradoxes of Irrationality." In *Philosophical Essays on Freud,* ed. Richard Wollheim and James Hopkins, 289–305. Cambridge: Cambridge University Press, 1982.

———. "What Metaphors Mean." In *Inquiries into Truth and Interpretation,* 245–64. Oxford: Clarendon, 1984.

Davis, Kathy. "Remaking the She-Devil: A Critical Look at Feminist Approaches to Beauty." *Hypatia* 6 (1991): 21–43.

Derrida, Jacques. "Avoir l'oreille de la philosophie." Interviewed by Lucette Finas. *La Quinzaine littéraire,* November 16, 1972, 13–16.

———. *De la grammatologie.* Paris: Minuit, 1967.

———. "La Différance." In *Marges de la philosophie,* 1–29. Paris: Minuit, 1972.

———. "La Dissémination." In *La Dissémination,* 321–407. Paris: Seuil, 1972.

———. *Glas.* Paris: Galilée, 1974.

———. "Limited Inc, a b c . . ." *Glyph* 2 (1977): 162–254.

———. "La Mythologie blanche." In *Marges de la philosophie,* 249–324. Paris: Minuit, 1972.

———. *Of Grammatology.* Translated by Gayatri Chakravorty Spivak. Baltimore: Johns Hopkins University Press, 1976.

———. "La pharmacie de Platon." In *La Dissémination,* 71–197. Paris: Seuil, 1972.

———. *Positions.* Paris: Minuit, 1972.

———. *Spurs: Nietzsche's Styles/Eperons: Les Styles de Nietzsche.* Bilingual ed. Translated by Barbara Harlow. Chicago: University of Chicago Press, 1979.

———. "La Structure, le signe et le jeu dans le discours des sciences humaines." In *L'Écriture et la différence,* 409–28. Paris: Seuil, 1967.

———. "This Strange Institution Called Literature: An Interview with Jacques Derrida." In *Jacques Derrida: Acts of Literature,* ed. Derek Attridge, 33–75. Interviewed by Derek Attridge, translated by Geoffrey Bennington and Rachel Bowlby. New York: Routledge, 1992.

———. *La vérité en peinture.* Paris: Flammarion, 1978.

Dykeman, Therese Boos, ed. *The Neglected Canon: Nine Women Philosophers, First to Twentieth Century.* Dordrecht: Kluwer, 1999.

Eagly, Alice H., and Valerie J. Steffen. "Gender and Aggressive Behavior: A Meta-analytic Review of the Social Psychological Literature." *Psychological Bulletin* 100 (1986): 309–30.

Elshtain, Jean Bethke. "Augustine and Diversity." In *A Catholic Modernity?* ed. James L. Heft, 97–102. New York: Oxford University Press 1999.

———. *Augustine and the Limits of Politics.* Notre Dame: University of Notre Dame Press, 1995.

———. "Contesting Care." *American Political Science Review* 88 (1994): 966–70.

———. "Ethics in the Women's Movement." In *Different Roles, Different Voices,* ed. Marianne Githens, Pippa Norris, and Joni Lovenduski, 233–44. New York: HarperCollins, 1994.

———. "Feminist Discourse and Its Discontents: Language, Power, and Meaning." *Signs* 7 (1982): 603–21.

———. "The New Feminist Scholarship." *Salmagundi* 70–71 (1986): 5–26.

———. *Power Trips and Other Journeys: Essays in Feminism as Civic Discourse.* Madison: University of Wisconsin Press, 1990.

———. *Public Man, Private Woman: Women in Social and Political Thought.* 2nd ed. Princeton: Princeton University Press, 1993.

———. *Women and War.* Chicago: University of Chicago Press, 1995.

Evans, J. Claude. *Strategies of Deconstruction: Derrida and the Myth of the Voice.* Minneapolis: University of Minnesota Press, 1991.

Fausto-Sterling, Anne. *Myths of Gender.* 2nd ed. New York: Basic Books, 1992.

Feyerabend, Paul. *Killing Time.* Chicago: University of Chicago Press, 1995.

Flax, Jane. "Political Philosophy and the Patriarchal Unconscious: A Psychoanalytical Perspective on Epistemology and Metaphysics." In *Discovering Reality: Feminist Perspectives on Epistemology, Metaphysics, Methodology, and the Philosophy of Science,* ed. Sandra Harding and Merrill B. Hintikka, 245–81. Dordrecht: Reidel, 1983.

Foucault, Michel. *Discipline and Punish: The Birth of the Prison.* Translated by Alan Sheridan. New York: Pantheon, 1977.

———. *History of Sexuality, Vol. 1.* Translated by Robert Hurley. New York: Pantheon, 1978.

Fox Keller, Evelyn. *Reflections on Gender and Science.* New Haven: Yale University Press, 1985.

Fox Keller, Evelyn, and Christine Grontkowski. "The Mind's Eye." In *Discovering Reality: Feminist Perspectives on Epistemology, Metaphysics, Methodology, and Philosophy of Science,* ed. Sandra Harding and Merrill B. Hintikka, 207–24. Dordrecht: Reidel, 1983.

Freire, Paulo. *Pedagogy of the Oppressed.* Translated by Myra Bergman Ramos. New York: Seabury Press, 1974.

Fricker, Miranda. "Feminism in Epistemology: Pluralism Without Postmodernism." In *The Cambridge Companion of Feminism in Philosophy,* ed. Miranda Fricker and Jennifer Hornsby, 146–65. Cambridge, Cambridge University Press, 2000.

Fricker, Miranda, and Jennifer Hornsby. "Introduction." In *The Cambridge Companion of Feminism in Philosophy,* ed. Miranda Fricker and Jennifer Hornsby, 1–9. Cambridge: Cambridge University Press, 2000.

Frye, Marilyn. *The Politics of Reality: Essays in Feminist Theory.* Trumansburg, N.Y.: Crossings Press, 1983.

Gatens, Moira. "The Feminist Critique of Philosophy." In *Feminism and Philosophy: Perspectives on Difference and Equality,* 85–97. Cambridge: Polity Press, 1991.

———. "Modern Rationalism." In *A Companion to Feminist Philosophy,* ed. Alison M. Jaggar and Iris Marion Young, 21–29. Malden, Mass.: Blackwell, 1998.

Gilligan, Carol. *In a Different Voice: Psychological Theory and Women's Development.* Cambridge: Harvard University Press, 1982.

Gilligan, Carol, and Jane Attanucci. "Much Ado About . . . Knowing? Noting? Nothing? A Reply to Vasudev Concerning Sex Differences and Moral Development." *Merrill-Palmer Quarterly* 34 (1988): 451–56.

———. "Two Moral Orientations: Gender Differences and Similarities." *Merrill-Palmer Quarterly* 34 (1988): 223–37.

Green, Judith M. "Aristotle on Necessary Verticality, Body Heat, and Gendered Proper Places in the Polis: A Feminist Critique." *Hypatia* 7 (1992): 70–96.

Griffin, Susan. *Woman and Nature: The Roaring Inside Her.* New York: Harper, 1980.

Griffiths, Morwenna, and Margaret Whitford. "Introduction." In *Feminist Perspectives in Philosophy,* ed. Morwenna Griffiths and Margaret Whitford, 1–28. London: Macmillan, 1988.

Grimshaw, Jean. *Philosophy and Feminist Thinking.* Minneapolis: University of Minnesota Press, 1986.

Gross, Elizabeth. "Conclusion: What is Feminist Theory?" In *Feminist Challenges: Social and Political Theory,* ed. Carole Pateman and Elizabeth Gross, 190–204. Boston: Northeastern University Press, 1987.

Haack, Susan. "The Best Man for the Job May Be a Woman . . . And Other Alien Thoughts on Affirmative Action in the Academy." In *Manifesto of a Passionate Moderate: Unfashionable Essays,* 167–87. Chicago: University of Chicago Press, 1998.

———. *Defending Science—Within Reason: Between Scientism and Cynicism.* Amherst, Mass.: Prometheus, 2003.

———. " 'Dry Truth and Real Knowledge': Epistemologies of Metaphor and Metaphors of Epistemology." In *Manifesto of a Passionate Moderate: Unfashionable Essays,* 69–89. Chicago: University of Chicago Press, 1998.

———. *Evidence and Inquiry: Towards Reconstruction in Epistemology.* Oxford: Blackwell, 1993.

———. "Knowledge and Propaganda: Reflections of an Old Feminist." In *Manifesto of a Passionate Moderate: Unfashionable Essays,* 123–36. Chicago: University of Chicago Press, 1998.

———. *Manifesto of a Passionate Moderate: Unfashionable Essays.* Chicago: University of Chicago Press, 1998.

———. "Science as Social?—Yes and No." In *Manifesto of a Passionate Moderate: Unfashionable Essays,* 124–22. Chicago: University of Chicago Press, 1998.

———. "Science 'From a Feminist Perspective.' " *Philosophy* 67 (1992): 5–18.

Hampton, Jean. "Feminist Contractarianism." In *A Mind of One's Own: Feminist Essays on Reason and Objectivity,* ed. Louise M. Antony and Charlotte Witt, 227–55. Boulder, Colo.: Westview Press, 1993.

Harding, Sandra. "Introduction: Is There a Feminist Method?" In *Feminism and Methodology*, ed. Sandra Harding, 1–14. Bloomington: Indiana University Press, 1987.

————. *The Science Question in Feminism*. Ithaca: Cornell University Press, 1986.

————. *Whose Science? Whose Knowledge?* Ithaca: Cornell University Press, 1991.

Harding, Sandra, and Merrill B. Hintikka. "Introduction." In *Discovering Reality: Feminist Perspectives on Epistemology, Metaphysics, Methodology, and Philosophy of Science,* ed. Harding and Hintikka, ix–xix. Dordrecht: Reidel, 1983.

Hartsock, Nancy. "Fundamental Feminism: Process and Perspective." In *Building Feminist Theory: Essays from "Quest," a Feminist Quarterly,* ed. Charlotte Bunch, Jane Flax, Alexa Freeman, Nancy Hartsock, and Mary-Helen Mautner, 32–43. New York: Longman, 1981.

————. *Money, Sex and Power: Toward a Feminist Historical Materialism*. New York: Longman, 1983.

Haslanger, Sally. "On Being Objective and Being Objectified." In *A Mind of One's Own: Feminist Essays on Reason and Objectivity,* ed. Louise M. Antony and Charlotte Witt, 85–125. Boulder, Colo.: Westview Press, 1993.

Hekman, Susan. "The Feminization of Epistemology: Gender and the Social Sciences." *Women and Politics* 7 (1987): 65–83.

Held, Virginia. *Feminist Morality: Transforming Culture, Society and Politics*. Chicago: University of Chicago Press, 1993.

Herman, Barbara. "Could It Be Worth Thinking About Kant on Sex and Marriage?" In *A Mind of One's Own: Feminist Essays on Reason and Objectivity,* ed. Louise M. Antony and Charlotte Witt, 49–67. Boulder, Colo.: Westview Press, 1993.

Hesse, Mary B. "The Cognitive Claims of Metaphor." *Journal of Speculative Philosophy* 2 (1988): 1–16.

————. *Models and Analogies in Science*. Notre Dame: University of Notre Dame Press, 1966.

Hintikka, Merrill B., and Jaakko Hintikka. "How Can Language Be Sexist?" In *Discovering Reality: Feminist Perspectives on Epistemology, Metaphysics, Methodology, and the Philosophy of Science,* ed. Sandra Harding and Merrill B. Hintikka, 139–48. Dordrecht: Reidel, 1983.

Hodge, Joanna. "Subject, Body and the Exclusion of Women from Philosophy." In *Feminist Perspectives in Philosophy,* ed. Morwenna Griffiths and Margaret Whitford, 152–70. London: Macmillan, 1988.

Hornsby, Jennifer. "Feminism in Philosophy of Language: Communicative Speech Acts." In *The Cambridge Companion of Feminism in Philosophy,* ed. Miranda Fricker and Jennifer Hornsby, 87–106. Cambridge: Cambridge University Press, 2000.

Hyde, Janet Shibley. "How Large Are Gender Differences in Aggression? A Developmental Meta-analysis." *Developmental Psychology* 20 (1984): 722–36.

Inglis, Laura Lyn, and Peter K. Steinfeld. *Old Dead White Men's Philosophy.* Amherst, N.Y.: Humanity Books, 2000.

Irigaray, Luce. "The Envelope: A Reading of Spinoza's *Ethics,* 'Of God.'" In *An Ethics of Sexual Difference,* trans. Carolyn Burke and Gillian C. Gill, 83–94. Ithaca: Cornell University Press, 1993.

———. *Speculum of the Other Woman.* Translated by Gillian Gill. Ithaca: Cornell University Press, 1985.

Jacklin, Carol Nagy. "Methodological Issues in the Study of Sex-Related Differences." *Developmental Review* 1 (1981): 266–73.

Jaffee, Sara, and Janet Shibley Hyde. "Gender Differences in Moral Orientation: A Meta-Analysis." *Psychological Bulletin* 126 (2000): 703–726.

Jaggar, Alison M. *Feminist Politics and Human Nature.* Totowa, N.J.: Rowman and Allenheld, 1983.

Jaggar, Alison M., and Iris Marion Young. "Introduction." In *A Companion to Feminist Philosophy,* ed. Jaggar and Young, 1–6. Oxford: Blackwell, 1998.

Kennedy, Ellen, and Susan Mendus, eds. *Women in Western Political Philosophy: Kant to Nietzsche.* Brighton: Wheatsheaf, 1987.

Le Doeuff, Michèle. "Women and Philosophy." In *French Feminist Thought,* edited by Toril Moi, translated by Debbie Pope, 181–209. Oxford: Blackwell, 1987.

Lernout, Geert. *The French Joyce.* Ann Arbor: University of Michigan Press, 1990.

Lewis, Bonnie Yegidis. "Psychological Factors Related to Wife Abuse." *Journal of Family Violence* 2 (1987): 1–10.

Linton, Rhoda. "Toward a Feminist Research Method." In *Gender/Body/Knowledge: Feminist Reconstructions of Being and Knowing,* ed. Alison M. Jaggar and Susan R. Bordo, 273–92. New Brunswick: Rutgers University Press, 1989.

Lloyd, Genevieve. "Feminism in History of Philosophy: Approaching the Past." In *The Cambridge Companion of Feminism in Philosophy,* ed. Miranda Fricker and Jennifer Hornsby, 245–63. Cambridge: Cambridge University Press, 2000.

———. "Maleness, Metaphor, and the 'Crisis' of Reason." In *A Mind of One's Own: Feminist Essays on Reason and Objectivity,* ed. Louise M. Antony and Charlotte Witt, 69–83. Boulder, Colo.: Westview Press, 1993.

———. *The Man of Reason: "Male" and "Female" in Western Philosophy.* 2nd ed. London: Routledge, 1993.

Longino, Helen. *Science as Social Knowledge.* Princeton: Princeton University Press, 1990.

Lorde, Audre. "The Master's Tools Will Never Dismantle the Master's House." In *Sister Outsider,* 110–13. Trumansburg, N.Y.: Crossings Press, 1984.

Louden, Robert B. *Kant's Impure Ethics: From Rational Beings to Human Beings.* New York: Oxford University Press, 2000.

———. "Kant's Virtue Ethics." *Philosophy* 61 (1986): 473–89.

Lovibond, Sabina. "Feminism and Pragmatism: A Reply to Richard Rorty." *New Left Review* 193 (1992): 56–74.

———. "Feminism and the 'Crisis of Rationality.'" *New Left Review* 207 (1994): 72–86.

Maccoby, Eleanor Emmons, and Carol Nagy Jacklin. *The Psychology of Sex Differences.* Stanford: Stanford University Press, 1974.

MacIntyre, Alasdair. *After Virtue.* Notre Dame: University Notre Dame Press, 1981.

———. *Whose Justice? Which Rationality?* Notre Dame: University Notre Dame Press, 1988.

MacKinnon, Catharine A. "Feminism, Marxism, Method and the State: An Agenda for Theory." *Signs* 7 (1982): 515–44.

———. "Feminism, Marxism, Method, and the State: Toward Feminist Jurisprudence." In *Feminism and Methodology,* ed. Sandra Harding, 135–156. Bloomington: Indiana University Press, 1987.

———. *Toward a Feminist Theory of the State.* Cambridge: Harvard University Press, 1989.

Mansbridge, Jane. "Feminism and Democratic Community." In *Democratic Community,* ed. John W. Chapman and Ian Shapiro, 339–95. New York: New York University Press, 1993.

McAlister, Linda Lopez, ed. *Hypatia's Daughters: Fifteen Hundred Years of Women Philosophers.* Bloomington: Indiana University Press, 1996.

Mendus, Susan. "How Androcentric Is Western Philosophy? A Reply." *Philosophical Quarterly* 46 (1996): 60–66.

———. "Kant: 'An Honest but Narrow-Minded Bourgeois'?" In *Immanuel Kant: Critical Assessments,* ed. Ruth F. Chadwick, vol. 3, 370–88. London: Routledge, 1992.

Merchant, Carolyn. *The Death of Nature: Women, Ecology, and the Scientific Revolution.* San Francisco: Harper, 1980.

Midgley, Mary. "Sex and Personal Identity: The Western Individualistic Tradition." *Encounter* 63, no. 1 (June 1984): 50–55.

Midgley, Mary, and Judith Hughes. *Women's Choices: Philosophical Problems Facing Feminism.* London: Weidenfeld and Nicolson, 1983.

Mies, Maria. "Towards a Methodology for Feminist Research." In *Theories of Women Studies,* ed. Gloria Bowles and Renate Duelli Klein, 117–39. London: Routledge, 1983.

Moody-Adams, Michele M. "Gender and the Complexity of Moral Voices." In *Feminist Ethics,* ed. Claudia Card, 195–212. Lawrence: University Press of Kansas, 1991.

Moulton, Janice. "A Paradigm of Philosophy: The Adversary Method." In *Women, Knowledge and Reality: Explorations in Feminist Philosophy,* 2nd ed., ed. Ann Garry and Marilyn Pearsall, 11–25. New York: Routledge, 1996.

Narayan, Uma. "The Project of Feminist Epistemology: Perspectives from a Nonwestern Feminist." In *Gender/Body/Knowledge: Feminist Reconstructions of Being and Knowing,* ed. Alison M. Jaggar and Susan R. Bordo, 256–59. New Brunswick: Rutgers University Press, 1989.

Nelson, Lynn Hankinson. *Who Knows: From Quine to a Feminist Empiricism.* Philadelphia: Temple University Press, 1990.

Noddings, Nel. *Caring: A Feminine Approach to Ethics and Moral Education.* Berkeley and Los Angeles: University of California Press, 1984.

Nozick, Robert. *Anarchy, State and Utopia.* Oxford: Basil Blackwell, 1974.

Nussbaum, Martha C. "Human Functioning and Social Justice: In Defense of Aristotelian Essentialism." *Political Theory* 20 (1992): 202–46.

———. "Feminists and Philosophy." *New York Review of Books,* October 20, 1994, 59–63.

———. "The Feminist Critique of Liberalism." In *Sex and Social Justice,* 55–80. Oxford: Oxford University Press, 1999.

O'Neill, Onora. "Kant After Virtue." *Inquiry* 26 (1984): 387–405.

Okin, Susan Moller. "Gender, the Public and the Private." In *Political Theory Today,* ed. David Held, 67–90. Cambridge: Polity Press, 1991.

———. *Justice, Gender and the Family.* New York: Basic Books, 1989.

———. "Reason and Feeling in Thinking About Justice." *Ethics* 99 (1989): 229–49.

———. "Sexual Orientation and Gender: Dichotomizing Differences." In *Sex, Preference and Family: Essays on Law and Nature,* ed. David M. Estlund and Martha C. Nussbaum, 44–59. New York: Oxford University Press, 1997.

———. *Women in Western Political Thought.* Princeton: Princeton University Press, 1992.

Pateman, Carole. "Introduction." In *Feminist Challenges: Social and Political Theory,* ed. Carole Pateman and Elizabeth Gross, 1–10. Boston: Northeastern University Press, 1987.

Perrett, Roy W. "Libertarianism, Feminism, and Relative Identity." *The Journal of Value Inquiry* 34 (2000): 383–95.

Phillips, Anne. *Democracy and Difference.* Cambridge: Polity Press, 1993.

Rawls, John. *A Theory of Justice.* Cambridge: Harvard University Press, 1971.

Richards, Janet Radcliffe. *The Sceptical Feminist: A Philosophical Enquiry.* 2nd ed. London: Penguin, 1994.

Rooney, Phyllis. "Gendered Reason: Sex Metaphor and Conceptions of Reason." *Hypatia* 6 (1991): 77–103.

Rorty, Richard. "Is Derrida a Transcendental Philosopher?" In *Derrida: A Critical Reader,* ed. David Wood, 235–46. Oxford: Blackwell, 1992.

Sandel, Michael J. *Liberalism and the Limits of Justice.* 2nd ed. Cambridge: Cambridge University Press, 1998.

Saxonhouse, Arlene W. *Women in the History of Political Thought: Ancient Greece to Machiavelli.* New York: Praeger, 1985.

Scanlon, John. "Pure Presence: A Modest Proposal." In *Derrida and Phenomenology,* ed. William R. McKenna and J. Claude Evans, 95–101. Dordrecht: Kluwer, 1995.

Schott, Robin May. "The Gender of Enlightenment." In *What Is Enlightenment? Eighteenth-Century Answers and Twentieth-Century Questions,* ed. James Schmidt, 471–487. Berkeley and Los Angeles: University of California Press, 1996.

———. "Resurrecting Embodiment: Toward a Feminist Materialism." In *A Mind of One's Own: Feminist Essays on Reason and Objectivity,* ed. Louise M. Antony and Charlotte Witt, 171–84. Boulder, Colo.: Westview Press, 1993.

Searle, John. "Metaphor." In *Metaphor and Thought,* ed. Andrew Ortony, 92–123. Cambridge: Cambridge University Press, 1979.

Soble, Alan. "Feminist Epistemology and Women Scientists." *Metaphilosophy* 14 (1983): 295–96.

———. "In Defense of Bacon." In *A House Built on Sand,* ed. Noretta Koertge, 195–215. New York: Oxford University Press, 1998. This is an expanded version of "In Defense of Bacon," *Philosophy of the Social Sciences* 25 (1995): 192–215.

Stuhlmacher, Alice, and Amy Walters. "Gender Differences in Negotiating Outcome: A Meta-Analysis." *Personnel Psychology* 52 (1999): 653–77.

Tanesini, Alessandra. *An Introduction to Feminist Epistemologies.* Oxford: Blackwell, 1999.

Thiele, Beverly. "Vanishing Acts in Social and Political Thought: Tricks of the Trade." In *Feminist Challenges: Social and Political Theory,* ed. Carole Pateman and Elizabeth Gross, 30–43. Boston: Northeastern University Press, 1987.

Thompson, Jana. "Women and the High Priests of Reason." *Radical Philosophy* 34 (1983): 10–14.

Tronto, Joan C. "Political Science and Caring: or, The Perils of Balkanized Social Science." *Women and Politics* 73 (1987): 85–97.

Tuana, Nancy. *Woman and the History of Philosophy.* St. Paul, Minn.: Paragon, 1992.

Vasudev, Jyotsna. "Sex Differences in Morality and Moral Orientation: A Discussion of the Gilligan and Attanucci Study." *Merrill Palmer Quarterly* 34 (1988): 239–44.

Vickers, Brian. "Derrida's Reading of C. S. Peirce." Letters to the Editor, *Times Literary Supplement,* May 9, 1997.

Waithe, Mary Ellen, ed. *A History of Women Philosophers.* 4 vols. Dordrecht: Kluwer, 1987–1995.

Warnock, Mary, ed. *Women Philosophers.* Everyman Library. London: J. M. Dent; Rutland, Vt.: Charles E. Tuttle, 1996.

Williams, Joan C. "Deconstructing Gender." *Michigan Law Review* 87 (1989): 797–845.

Wilshire, Donna. "The Uses of Myth, Image, and the Female Body in Re-visioning Knowledge." In *Gender/Body/Knowledge: Feminist Reconstructions of Being and Knowing,* edited by Alison M. Jaggar and Susan R. Bordo, 92–114. New Brunswick: Rutgers University Press, 1989.

Young, Iris Marion. *Inclusion and Democracy.* New York: Oxford University Press, 2000.

Young-Bruehl, Elisabeth. "The Education of Women as Philosophers." In *Reconstructing the Academy: Women's Education and Women's Studies,* ed. Elizabeth Minnich, Jean O'Barr, and Rachel Rosenfeld, 9–23. Chicago: University of Chicago Press, 1988.

Index

individuation, 120. *See also* justice perspective

Inglis, Laura Lyn, 2, 147
interests, 93–102, 129
internal-external distinction, 38
Irigaray, Luce, 4, 55, 81

Jacklin, Carol Nagy, 105–7, 108
Jaggar, Alison M., 1, 147–48, 151, 155 n. 21
    on social reality and knowledge, 94–95, 98
Jainism, 43 n. 15
Jesus, 119
Jews, 37, 134
Joyce, James, 50
justice perspective, 103, 107–11, 117–20, 124–25, 150

Kant, Immanuel, 8, 61, 62 n. 8, 120, 128
    explicit androcentric statements in, 3, 14–15, 16, 26–29
Kennedy, Ellen, 13
Kierkegaard, Søren, 38, 120, 157–58

Lacan, Jacques, 54
Le Doeuff, Michèle, 42, 56
Leibniz, Gottfried Wilhelm, 120
Lernout, Greet, 50
lesbian families, 143–44
Leucippus, 51
liberalism, 132, 139–42
libertarianism, 135–39
Linton, Rhoda, 154–55
Lloyd, Genevieve, 1, 4, 5 n. 11, 13, 160
    arguments from associations, stereotypes, and social practices, 31–41, 49
Locke, John, 13, 38, 82–83, 88, 128
logical positivism, 157–58. *See also* analytic philosophy
logocentrism, 43–54
Lorde, Audre, 4, 149
Louden, Robert B., 26–27, 120
Lovibond, Sabina, 5 n. 10, 56, 58
Lyotard, Jean-François, 54

Maccoby, Eleanor Emmons, 105–7
MacIntyre, Alasdair, 131, 132–35, 142–44
MacKinnon, Catharine, 4, 160
    on feminist methodology, 148, 151–52
    on metaphors, 75–80, 81

on objectivity and objectification, 60–61, 64, 66–67
manipulation. *See* control
Mansbridge, Jane, 145
Marcel, Gabriel, 120
Marcus Aurelius, 121 n. 37
Marxist analysis, 94–95, 98, 129–30
McAlister, Linda Lopez, 96 n. 6
Mendus, Susan, 4, 13, 16, 27–28
Merchant, Caroline, 72–74
Merleau-Ponty, Maurice, 76
metaphors, 32 n. 1, 71–91, 160, 163
    interactionist theory of, 84–87
    network theory of, 84–85
    substitution theory of, 84–87
    visual, 74–80
methodology, 147–58
Midgley, Mary, 8 nn. 17, 18
Mies, Maria, 149
Mill, John Stuart, 120
Moody-Adams, Michele M., 107, 108, 110 n. 13
Moulton, Janice, 122–24
Muslims, 100, 134
mystical knowledge, 77, 78, 151

Narayan, Uma, 148 n. 5
nature, 58–60
    arguments from, 114
    in Aristotle, 18, 22–24
    in Bacon, 72–74
    in Derrida, 51, 52
    mystical ability to connect with, 151
Nelson, Lynn Hankinson, 72 n. 2
neutrality, 62–69, 101–2 n. 13, 118
Nietzsche, Friedrich, 14, 15, 38, 99, 157–58
Noddings, Nel, 103, 117–18
Nozick, Robert, 131, 135–39, 142–44
Nussbaum, Martha C., 5 n. 10, 39, 58–59, 148–49

objectification, 60–69, 75–80, 160
objectivity, 60–69, 74–80, 95, 160. *See also* justice perspective
Oedipal complex, 81–82
Okin, Susan Moller, 13, 120, 148 n. 3
    arguments from omission, 128, 130–46
    on Aristotle, 17–22
    employment of the term "deconstruction," 52 n. 45
    on Rousseau, 17, 24–25

vision, 74–80
vote, women's, 37, 59, 112–13
   in Kant 3, 26, 28

Waithe, Mary Ellen, 96 n. 6
Walzer, Michael, 131, 143 n. 11
Weininger, Otto, 115
welfare, 129, 136
Whitford, Margaret, 1
will, 132–33

Williams, Joan C., 52 n. 45, 107
Wilshire, Donna, 35 n. 6, 37 n. 7
witches, 72–74
Wittgenstein, Ludwig, 44
Wolgast, Elizabeth, 28
women's empowerment, 39–40, 59,
   164–65
wordplay, 46–47, 53–54

Young, Iris Marion, 1, 145
Young-Bruehl, Elisabeth, 58